GROWING IN GRACE

Bob George

HARVEST HOUSE PUBLISHERS
Eugene, Oregon 97402

Cover by Terry Dugan Design, Minneapolis, Minnesota

GROWING IN GRACE with Study Guide

Copyright © 1991 by Harvest House Publishers
Eugene, Oregon 97402

Library of Congress Cataloging-in-Publication Data

George, Bob, 1933–
    [Growing in grace]
    Growing in grace with study guide / Bob George.
        p.   cm.
    Originally published as two separate titles: Growing in grace and Growing in grace study guide. 1991.
    ISBN 1-56507-697-4
    1. Grace (Theology)—Popular works.   2. Christian life—Study and teaching.   I. George, Bob, 1933–
    Growing in grace study guide.   II. Title.
    BT761.2.G46   1997   97-2657
    248.4—dc21   CIP

Printed in the United States of America.

97   98   99   00   01   02   03   / BC /   10   9   8   7   6   5   4   3   2   1

Contents

A Personal Note from the Author

You and I have a great deal in common.

Although we have probably never met, I can positively guarantee that we have been to the same school. The school I am referring to is the "school of performance."

Shakespeare once said, "All the world is a stage and all the men and women merely players." From the beginning we are taught that we must perform properly in order to get what we want. A direct correlation exists between how hard we work and how much we are rewarded.

"Be good and you'll get a cookie."

"Clean your room and you'll get your allowance."

"Practice hard and you'll make the varsity team."

"Lose weight and you'll get more dates."

"Study in college and you'll get a better job."

"Make more money and you'll be happier."

And on and on it goes.

The tragedy of this world's philosophy is that we become so conditioned by it that we carry it over into our Christian experience. The grace of God that saves us loses its meaning as we are bombarded with the pressure to perform.

This pressure often comes packaged in Christian verbiage such as "God helps those who help themselves." It sounds good; the only problem is that it's not biblical!

There is one and only one place where you and I can stop performing—in the unconditional love and acceptance of Jesus Christ. The same grace that saves us is what sustains us. It teaches us how to live here and now ... without performing.

In my first book, *Classic Christianity*, I shared many of the biblical truths that enable people to escape from spiritual bondage to enjoy the freedom that is found in Jesus Christ. It has been thrilling to receive the hundreds of letters and calls from people who have been set free to know and love their Lord as never before. The achievement of liberty is one thing; learning to live as a free man or woman is something else. After the joyful experience of breaking out of former captivity comes the inevitable need to learn how to deal with freedom. Those who have been saved by grace and set free by grace must now learn how to grow in grace.

That is the purpose of this book. In *Classic Christianity* I laid the foundation for the Christian's understanding of his identity in Christ, of total forgiveness of sins, of righteousness through Him, and of receiving Christ's resurrected life. The emphasis of the first book is to share truth that sets people free in Christ. In this book my primary aim is to give Christians who are beginning to experience their freedom in Christ the necessary understanding to grow in His grace as beloved children of God.

The stories and counseling situations shared in this book are true, with the names changed in some instances to protect the individuals' privacy. As they are reproduced in this volume, the problems, progress, and resolutions faithfully depict those situations as they happened, though these are not literal transcripts of conversations.

For years I have observed Christians who are tired of "acting like Christians," of going through the meaningless motions, and of putting on their hypocritical masks. To those who have grown weary and heavy-laden the Lord Jesus made His appeal, "Come unto *ME* . . . . and I will give you rest" (Matthew 11:28 NASB).

To those of you who have given it all you've got trying to meet an impossible standard, trying to live up to the image of the phantom "good Christian," trying your best to please God only to make the hollow discovery that it isn't enough; there is hope in the pages to come.

It is my prayer that the Holy Spirit will use His Word and the biblical truths illustrated in this book to enable you to fully experience Christ's resurrected life, to enjoy and rejoice in the liberty that He has purchased for you by His blood, and to grow you in His wonderful grace.

—Bob George

ONE

◈

Real Life in the Real World

I had been a Christian for about six years, and had come to Dallas to head up a major citywide evangelistic campaign. I was working with some of the largest churches in America, hosting a daily radio program, and coordinating our efforts with local television stations. The atmosphere was "continuous excitement," and I was right in the center of it all. I was beginning to think I was very close to reaching the ultimate in Christian maturity . . . until one day I took my wife, Amy, shopping.

It was a crowded, busy day at the shopping center, and it was hard to find a parking space. Therefore I thought it was my lucky day when I found not *one* but *two* empty spaces right in front of the store we wanted! But just as I was approaching my "answer-to-prayer" parking space, a guy driving a shiny new foreign car pulled into that spot and straddled the line, taking up both spaces.

At first I thought it was an accident. I rolled down my window and said nicely, "Sir, you probably haven't noticed, but you've taken up two spaces."

He just gave me a quick glance and said with a smirk, "I know it." As he got out of his car I got a good look at him. He was middle-aged, with flecks of gray in his well-coiffed hair. His shirt was open down the front, revealing numerous gold chains dangling over what looked like a "chest toupee."

I felt instant and total dislike for that man. A little more forcefully I responded, "Well, would you please repark it, so I can use one of the spaces?" Holding out his arm to escort a much younger-looking girl, he replied, "No."

At that moment all those years of being a child of God didn't mean a thing to me. My mood was now murderous. "Buddy," I said through clenched teeth, "if you don't move that car I'm going to stuff you in the tailpipe and move it for you!" I started to get out of my car, fully intending to do what I said.

Amy looked at me as if I'd lost my mind, and said so. I told her that it wasn't my *mind* that I was worried about losing; it was that parking space! Suddenly I stopped. "What are you doing?" I asked myself. "You were perfectly willing—in fact, excited—to give up your thriving, lucrative business to go into full-time ministry, but you are ready to fight another person rather than give up that parking space!"

Having finally come to my senses, I spent the next several minutes maneuvering my car through the lot, driving mostly in reverse. My goal was to keep the guy with the foreign car from seeing my rear bumper—the one with the sticker that said "Smile! Jesus loves you."

Have you ever been there? In spite of a sincere and genuine faith in Jesus Christ, have you ever suddenly found yourself acting in a stupid manner, as if you never heard of the gospel? If we were totally honest, we would all admit to such times. All of us can forget who we are and what we believe in an unexpected moment. We've all heard the voices, either real or imagined: "I thought you were a Christian!" comes the sneer. "I thought I was too," we respond in disgust. "How could I do such a thing?"

Let's be a little more pointed. Besides "unexpected moments," we all know that Christians can choose to live in a determined and long-term manner that is contrary to what God's Word says. In fact, we all have areas of our lives where we face ongoing struggles with temptation and failure. We sometimes wonder if we'll *ever* begin making progress in this Christian life. Every believer I have ever known—with the possible exception of those who are brand-new in the faith—has experienced what the apostle Paul described: "I do not understand what I do. For what I want to do I do not do, but what I hate I do. . . . For I have the desire to do what is good, but I cannot carry it out. For what I do is not the good I want to do; no, the evil I do not want to do—this I keep on doing" (Romans 7:15,18,19).

This same conflict has been experienced by Christians of all ages, from every denomination, and from every geographical region. They've been put on guilt trips and brow-beaten to give it everything they've got, but in spite of their sincere efforts, it just isn't enough. Simply put, what we need is *life*. And that is exactly what Jesus Christ offers us: "I have come that they may have *life*, and have it to the full" (John 10:10).

In my book *Classic Christianity*, my aim is to help us as Christians return to the living Christ as our life—and not just for "help" to live the Christian life, and not for some impersonal infusion of "power," and not for some magic formula that will cause our lives to "click" and become all smooth sailing; no, Jesus Christ *is* our life! "For you died, and your life is now hidden with Christ in God. When *Christ, who is your life,* appears, then you also will appear with Him in glory" (Colossians 3:3,4).

In that book we survey the amazing inheritance that belongs to every child of God because of our identification with Jesus Christ. As Peter says, "His divine power has given us *everything we need for life and godliness* through our knowledge of Him who called us by His own glory and goodness" (2 Peter 1:3). Therefore the Christian life is not "starting out" with Jesus and then "graduating" to something better. There is no such thing as "advanced Christianity"; every person who begins his Christian life begins it with everything he will ever receive.

To use an illustration carried over from *Classic Christianity,* it reminds me of the apples that could be found all over the part of Indiana where I grew up. During the early spring those apple trees bore fruit that was small, unappetizing, and hard as a brick—so hard, in fact, that we kids had a great time having wars with them. I still remember the abiding satisfaction of really clobbering one of my friends in the head with one of those apples. The point I'm making is this: What was the nature of those small, hard fruits? They weren't watermelons, and they weren't pumpkins. No, they were 100 percent *apples.* They were not very edible, and they were as hard as rocks, but they were still totally apple. Their nature would not change as they grew, nor would they gain anything that was not already there. They would simply *mature.*

This is the answer to the questions that people ask in response to verses like 2 Peter 1:3, quoted above. "How could a person who has been given 'everything he needs for life and godliness' continue to struggle? What more can we need when we already have 'everything'?"

Simply this: Even though we were given everything we will ever need at our spiritual birth, we still have *a whole lifetime of growing in our understanding of Christ* and of the riches, power, and life that He has already given us! This is why the apostle Peter wrote:

> But *grow in the grace* and knowledge of our Lord and Savior Jesus Christ. To Him be glory both now and forever! (2 Peter 3:18).

If you're tired of giving it all you've got and still coming up short, this book is for you. We will look at various angles of real life in the real world and see how Jesus Christ living in us provides the answers. We'll see how growing in grace is not a matter of *our* becoming bigger and stronger *in and of ourselves,* but of simply getting ourselves out of the way and *allowing Christ to live His life* in and through us.

I should first point out what growing in grace is *not*. This book is not going to present "ten steps to spirituality" or provide a ladder by which you can "climb to Christian character in 12 easy steps." That is one of our major hindrances today: the unrealistic belief that growing in grace is simply the mastering of certain "principles." *We have approached the Christian life as a subject to be learned rather than as a life to be lived.* You can't grow in grace in a classroom, through a seminar, or during a "quiet time," as good as those things may be. As a matter of fact, you cannot grow in grace through reading a book, not even this one. You can only grow in grace through a personal relationship with the Lord Jesus Christ, who teaches you truth from His Word, which you then take out into the rough-and-tumble of real life in the real world.

The "curriculum" cannot be planned or anticipated. Through the sovereignty of a loving God, the pathway we will tread in this fallen world will be as unique as each one of us. Along the way in this book we'll meet many individuals whose lives demonstrate how God can grow us in grace regardless of the circumstances we may encounter.

J.E. was a hard man who left a trail of resentments and hurts in his family relationships. Late in life he heard about the forgiveness of sins and the life that is found in Jesus Christ, and his life was transformed. Then he learned that he had terminal lung cancer. If J.E. were going to grow in grace, it would have to be under the pressure of knowing that he had only a short time to live.

Gary grew up in an abusive home with an alcoholic father. His mother ran away when he was four. By the time he was in his teens, he had already become an alcoholic and serious drug-user. According to his own admission, every four-letter word imaginable was tattooed somewhere on his body. Under the influence of drugs one night, he and another man seriously beat two hitchhikers and robbed them. He was sentenced to prison, where he heard the gospel and was born again. If Gary were going to grow in grace, he had to begin in prison.

In later chapters of this book I will tell you how the stories of J.E. and Gary turned out.

Accounts of real people like these remind us of the truth of Jesus' statement "In this world you will have trouble" (John 16:33). If growing in grace required perfect conditions, it would never happen, since we grow in the midst of real life. Remember that millions of Christians, both in the past and in this century, have lived under severe government persecution. If believers under hostile governments are going to grow in grace, it will be under those conditions.

But not all examples are drastic or involve what we would call tragedy. Everyday life consists of an incredible variety of lifestyles. I think of Billy Graham, for example, with his huge worldwide ministry. A man in Dr. Graham's position will have to grow in grace in that kind of fishbowl existence. A businessman will have to grow in grace in the often viciously competitive business world. High school students will have to grow in grace under the challenging conditions of growing up physically and socially amid strong peer pressure. Many people have been privileged to live in happy families. They will have to grow in grace in the midst of a "Leave It to Beaver" type of household.

Whatever the situations in *your* life may be, *that* is where you will have to grow in grace.

Another aspect of growth that people often miss is this: We grow in grace in spite of our personal failures and sins. How? *As we focus on what God is doing in the midst of what we are doing.* Hebrews 12:1,2 tells us:

> Let us throw off everything that hinders and the sin that so easily entangles, and let us run with perseverance the race marked out for us. *Let us fix our eyes on Jesus*, the author and perfecter of our faith, who for the joy set before Him endured the cross, scorning its shame, and sat down at the right hand of the throne of God.

Christ should be our concentration. On the other hand, if the focus is on *ourselves*, the result is predictable. Jesus Christ said:

> I am the vine; you are the branches. If a man remains in Me
> and I in him, he will bear much fruit; *apart from Me you can
> do nothing* (John 15:5).

Jesus said that He is the vine and we are branches. A branch
has no capacity at all to produce fruit or to grow itself. The vine
is the source of fruit, and it is the vine which grows the branch.
The branch's role is to "abide" or "remain" in the vine, meaning
that it continues in dependent relationship as it allows the life
of the vine to flow through it unhindered. In the parking lot
that day I demonstrated how much of Christ's life I can produce apart from total dependency on Him: None! As I often
say, the Christian life is not merely *hard* but *impossible!* Only
Christ can live it, and so the only intelligent thing we can do is
to let Him!

However, we all can and will take back the control of our
lives at times, thereby demonstrating once more our total
inability to bear the life of Christ on our own. The good news
is that the Lord knows all this about us but still accepts us. It is
not a shock to Him when we sin. When we "fix our eyes on
Jesus," we are focusing on a Person who is described as having
"glory, the glory of the One and Only, who came from the
Father, *full of grace and truth*" (John 1:14). When we sin, His *grace*
says, "*Neither do I condemn you*" (John 8:11). Then His Truth
says, "Let Me show you a better way," and points the way to
freedom: "If you abide in My word, then you are truly disciples
of mine; and you shall know the truth, and *the truth shall make
you free*" (John 8:31,32 NASB). God in His infinite grace and cre-
ativity takes even our weaknesses and failures and causes them
"to work together for good for those who love God, to those
who are called according to His purpose" (Romans 8:28 NASB).
When I was a brand-new Christian, I had an experience which

has stood in my life as a vivid example of God's patient but persistent work in our lives to cause us to grow in grace.

Before I became a believer, I worked as a sales manager for a large firm owned by a man named Bernie. He and I couldn't stand each other. But he kept me because I made him a lot of money, and I stayed because he paid me a lot of money. Back then we often had sales promotions in which we gave away merchandise to customers. One day during one of those campaigns I was down in the basement and noticed a stack of boxes containing Teflon pots and pans that we were giving away. Thinking that Amy would like them and figuring that Bernie would never know the difference, I took a box (I believe "stole" is the biblical word).

A few years later I became the owner of my own business in competition with Bernie. This thrilled me beyond measure because it gave me the opportunity to wipe Bernie out of business.

However, it wasn't long after getting my own business that I became a Christian. One day I was praying that God would reveal areas of my life that He wanted to work on. I couldn't believe what He brought to my mind.

I had asked God, "Show me anything in my life that You want me to do and I'll do it." I never heard an audible voice, but the message I received in reply could not have been clearer. The answer was, "Go tell Bernie about the pots and pans."

My heart dropped like a brick. I prayed, "O Lord, is there *anything else* you would like for me to do?" How could anything be so ridiculous as for me to go back to a sworn enemy and admit to stealing *pots and pans* from him? For months I tried to forget about it, but the thought would not go away. Every time I got quiet and prayed, Bernie came to my mind. I pled with the

Lord, "Lord, if only I'd stolen something worthwhile, it wouldn't be so bad! If only I'd stolen a car or a television set—anything but *pots and pans.*" It just seemed so wimpy and unmanly. All I could picture was humiliation if I followed through on the thought.

But God had reached into my life with His love and grace, and I was not the same man who once hated Bernie. As I thought back to when we worked together, I could see myself more truthfully. I had been in spiritual darkness at the time, but the Lord had brought me into His kingdom of light. I could now see that a large percentage of the problems between us back then were my own fault. Having been in darkness myself, I could symphathize with him. I was experiencing the change in attitudes spoken of in Titus 3:2-5, where it says that we ought—

> to slander no one, to be peaceable and considerate, and to show true humility toward all men. *At one time we too were foolish*, disobedient, deceived and enslaved by all kinds of passions and pleasures. We lived in malice and envy, being hated and hating one another. But when the kindness and love of God our Savior appeared, He saved us, not because of righteous things we had done, but because of His mercy.

I began to picture Bernie as a person for whom Christ also died. But Bernie had never heard the good news about "the kindness and love of God our Savior." In spite of my embarrassment, and in spite of the rocky history of Bernie's and my relationship, God wanted me to tell Bernie about the pots and pans. It didn't make much sense to me, but I couldn't deny that I knew what God was telling me to do. About six months passed before I finally called Bernie and asked him to lunch. He was quite surprised, but responded, "Sure, Bob."

We went out that day, and I discovered what a great conversationalist I could really be in a pinch! We talked politics, sports, business, and the latest jokes for a long, enjoyable lunch. In fact, we talked about practically every subject I could think of *except* the pots and pans!

We rode back to my office in Bernie's car, and I knew I had not done what I really wanted to do. Bernie parked and thanked me for the lunch, acting as if he had thoroughly enjoyed himself. I opened the car door and had one foot outside when I sighed and got back in. "Bernie," I said. "There's something else I want to say. Do you remember that time a few years ago when we had the promotion with the pots and pans?" "Yes," he answered. "Well, Bernie, back then I stole a set of those pots and pans from you, and I want to write you out a check for them right now."

Bernie was astonished—not just because someone would confess to having stolen from him, but especially because he couldn't believe that someone had been able to steal from him without his knowledge and want to pay it back!

After writing the check, I continued: "And Bernie, there's something else. Since the time I worked for you, I have come to know Jesus Christ as my Lord and Savior. And I'd like to tell you about Him and what I've learned." Bernie was open and interested, and we proceeded to discuss how Christ had changed my life. I told Bernie how sorry I was, not only for stealing from him (about 20 dollars in value), but more so for being so disrespectful to the one for whom I worked and who paid my salary. None of the humiliating scenes that I had spent months imagining came true. Instead, that time of sharing with Bernie was warm, friendly, and meaningful. I went back to my office that day rejoicing and praising God for His ongoing teaching ministry in my life—and wondering as well why I had needed several months to decide that He knows what He is doing and to trust Him!

Was God really that interested in pots and pans? Absolutely not. He was interested in my pride.

There is a lot of superficial Bible teaching that would say that I was "out of fellowship with God" during all those months I was resisting God's direction. Some would say that I could have no "power in witnessing" and that my prayers were surely "bouncing off the ceiling." "After all, God could not have communion with a disobedient Christian, could He?"

Ridiculous! God knew that it was going to take that much time for me to grow in grace to the point where I was willing to step out and trust Him with Bernie. In the meantime He was revealing Himself to me in a wonderful way, teaching me great things out of His Word, and using me to lead dozens of people to Christ—*all in the midst* of my unwillingness to trust Him in this one area of my life.

There is a type of teaching which says that a believer is either a "spiritual" (trusting, obedient) Christian or a "carnal" (unbelieving, disobedient) Christian—one or the other, 100 percent. In my opinion, that approach is unbiblical and unrealistic. There is no such thing as a Christian who is trusting God 100 percent in *every* area of his life. Each one of us has some areas that we have learned to trust the Lord in. But right alongside of these are other areas which we have not yielded, often without even being aware of it. For example, I may be trusting God in the areas of my marriage, children, and ministry, while at the same time I am living in self-sufficiency in the areas of my finances and leisure time. Over a lifetime, growing in grace involves God's opening our eyes to our need to trust Him in new areas of our lives, or on a new level of challenge, and then walking us through the process of learning to turn these areas over to Him.

Only this realistic view of growth can account for experiences like mine, where I was undeniably growing in my knowledge of the Lord Jesus Christ *at the same time* that I was not yet ready to present to Him an area of my life that He wanted to deal with. This is what I meant by the phrase used earlier: *If we are going to grow in grace, we must focus on what God is doing in the midst of what we are doing.* Let's face it—if God were waiting around for us to "root all known sin out of our lives" before beginning the process of growing us in His grace, *we would never grow!*

In this process, one of the major truths that the Lord always directs us to is our *identity in Him.* On the day I wanted to stuff that man in his tailpipe, God immediately worked in my heart, reasoning with me, "Bob, *who are you?*"

"I'm Your child, Lord," I thought.

"What does that mean, Bob?"

"It means that I'm totally acceptable to You, Lord. That all my sins are forgiven, even this one. And that I stand in the righteousness of Christ. He is in me and I am in Him."

"My son, in light of that, what sense does it make to lose your temper over a parking space? Which is more important, experiencing My life in you, or defending your own pride? Do you think I could possibly provide another parking space for you, not to mention anything else you need in this life?"

It surely seemed silly now. "Of course You can, Lord."

"Then remember who you are, and think of all the riches you have in Me. Trust Me." And I did.

In the light of who I am in Christ, what sense *does* it make to act like that? None at all! The wonderful thing about the grace of God is that none of this reasoning is for the purpose of condemnation. It is simply to remind us of *who we really are* so that we can return to dependency upon Him. I had been a butterfly who lapsed for a while back to acting like a worm. The message was simple: "Get up and fly." It was the same thing during the pots-and-pans episode. Even though I didn't have the understanding that I do today, I can look back and see that God was reasoning with me in the same way. "Who are you?" He continually asks us. Then He tells us to return to dependency upon Him and act in accordance with our true identity

The believer's identity in Christ is a truth that we will find ourselves coming back to again and again as we grow in grace. Even though we laid a firm foundation of this truth in *Classic Christianity*, we will reemphasize it often in this book. *We never outgrow our need to be reminded of who we are in Christ!* It is something that God is trying to teach us from the first day of our Christian lives until the day we go home to heaven, and this truth provides a constant standard against which we learn to measure our thinking and responses throughout life.

Another major truth which provides a track for our journey is our life of *dependent faith in the living Christ*. When Jesus said, "Apart from Me you can do nothing," He meant exactly what He said. The point which many Christians fail to grasp is that this statement applies to our lives both before *and after* receiving Christ! It is sometimes a hard lesson to learn, but I can speak from personal experience: It is worth it! Jesus said, *"The truth will set you free"* (John 8:32). Truth is not always pleasant to hear, but truth will always set you free when you abide in it by faith in the living Christ. The same Word which tells us "Apart from

Me you can do nothing" also says "I can do everything through him who gives me strength" (Philippians 4:13). The key words are *through Him*. That is diametrically opposed to a life of *self*-improvement, *self*-development, or *self*-control.

In spite of the fact that we have been given "everything we need for life and godliness" and have actually become "partakers of the divine nature" through the indwelling Holy Spirit (2 Peter 1:3, 4 NASB), we still at times approach life in an attitude of self-sufficiency, as if we have no other resource for living. It can happen to any of us at any time. We can be doctrinally correct Christians yet live as practical atheists. But what do I mean by the term practical atheist? There is an old illustration that describes this attitude vividly.

Imagine that you are driving a pickup truck down a road when you meet a hitchhiker carrying an immense pack on his back. You feel real compassion for this man, bent under this giant load on such a hot day, so you decide to help him. You pull over and offer him a ride, which he gratefully accepts. He climbs onto the back of your truck, and you resume driving.

A little way down the road you look in the mirror and see an incredible sight. There the hitchhiker sits, hunched over, *still holding on to his huge pack*. You pull over again and say, "Hey, buddy, why don't you put that pack down on the bed of the truck?"

His response is, "That's okay. I don't want to bother you that much. Just take me to my destination and I'll be grateful."

So off you go, with the hitchhiker riding in the back, still shouldering his burden.

Many of us approach the Christian life in the same way. We happily accept the Lord's offer of help, and board His "salvation wagon" that will take us to heaven. But in the meantime *we* bear our own burdens on the way there, in spite of such biblical promises as "cast all your anxiety on Him because He cares for you" (1 Peter 5:7). Jesus did not come just to deal with your eternal destiny while leaving you on your own to deal with daily living. *Jesus Christ laid down His life for you so that He could give His life to you so that He could live His life through you!*

After repeated failure to live the Christian life on our own, many of us have lost hope of ever experiencing the reality of the Lord's wonderful promise: "I have come that they may have life, and have it to the full" (John 10:10). I want to restore that hope! However, that fullness of life can only be experienced as we learn how to grow in grace. The good news is that growing in grace is not only *possible*, but it is God's *desire* for us. We can truly know a life of reality and love through abiding in Christ, the vine. It doesn't come through some dramatic experience, "total commitment," or magic prayer. It is a life that we grow in, and growing takes time. It is a *journey*, a *process* of growth that takes a lifetime, but God will continue to work on us until we are perfectly "conformed to the likeness of His Son" (Romans 8:29). In the meantime, as we grow, life presents us countless proofs—reminders—that God still has a lot of building to do in us. Usually these reminders come through those unexpected tests where we fall flat on our face, such as my parking lot encounter.

In order to grow in grace, we have to be willing to break out of a mindset that permeates American culture: Over the past few decades we have become a totally vicarious society—we prefer our experiences secondhand. We no longer go out and play a sport, such as baseball, basketball, or football. Instead we sit at home and watch a few people play it on television. Kids would rather play a video game where they zap villains for hours on end than run and play with other children. Millions of people would rather seek ideal love and relationships through romance novels or soap operas on television than mix it up with real people in real relationships, where they have faults and irritating qualities as well as attractive points.

I believe that many people have brought those same tendencies over into the Christian life. We want to study the Bible and learn untold amounts of minute details *about* the Scriptures rather than *applying* the truth we learned *in* the Scriptures. We want to read books *about* the Christian life rather than venturing out into the risky activity of *living* it. But as I said before, the Christian life is not a subject to be learned but a life to be lived! God will indeed teach us truth out of His Word as we dig into the Bible. "Do you see what the Bible *says?*" the Lord asks. "Yes," we answer. "Then fasten your seat belt," He replies, "because now I am going to show you what it means!" And He shows us what it *means* in the midst of everyday life. In a real sense, each of us is one-on-one with the Lord. No one else can live life for us. Each one of us must go to Him and individually grow in grace as He leads.

As we go, it is imperative that we keep our primary focus not on *growing* as such but on *Him* personally. In total sincerity we can put our emphasis in the wrong place. We want to "abide in Christ," which is biblical and proper. However, our emphasis can be "*abide* in Christ" rather than "abide in *Christ.*" We can become preoccupied and obsessive trying to figure out how to "abide" rather than focusing on the Person that we are abiding in. "Living by faith in Christ" is a proper objective—assuming that we are not concentrating on "living by *faith* in Christ" but on "living by faith in *Christ.*" We can make ourselves nervous wrecks by worrying about how much faith we have and trying to conjure up more, while totally missing Him who is the *object* of our faith. We can easily try to "grow in grace" by concentrating on *growing* at the expense of focusing on *Him* "who is *full of grace* and truth." We are called first and foremost to a *Person*.

In describing the ministries of himself and Apollos, Paul wrote, "I planted the seed, Apollos watered it, *but God made it grow*" (1 Corinthians 3:6). I am writing *Growing in Grace*—and I pray you are reading it—in the full recognition that this book cannot *make* you grow in grace. In fact, you cannot make *yourself* grow. *God* causes the growth! But He has promised us that "He who began a good work in you will carry it on to completion until the day of Christ Jesus" (Philippians 1:6). He wants to fill our minds with the knowledge of His love for us so that we will freely present ourselves back to Him to allow Him to work out His plan in our lives.

> Now to Him who is able to do *immeasurably more than all we ask or imagine, according to His power that is at work within us*, to Him be glory in the church and in Christ Jesus throughout all generations, for ever and ever! (Ephesians 3:20,21).

There is good news and great encouragement in the chapters ahead. My prayer for you is that God will open the eyes of your heart to enable you to understand His love and grace toward you, so you will discover truly abundant life as you grow in His wonderful grace.

TWO

Called
to a Person

When I was in high school, I was once hired for the summer as a farm worker. I'm sure this doesn't sound too thrilling, but I was extremely excited to have a real paying job. Just as a beautiful dawn was breaking, I piled onto the back of a truck with several other temporary workers and was driven out to the fields for my first day of work. That day our assignment was to hoe the tomato section. Our supervisor took a hoe and very carefully explained what we were to do. Certain weeds tended to grow around the tomato plants, so we were to go down the rows with our tools, clearing away the weeds.

My father had always impressed upon us the importance and value of hard work, so I attacked my new job with a vengeance. I was determined to be the best worker they had. I worked hard all morning, pushing myself to continue through the fatigue. And so it was with a sense of great satisfaction, as well as several new aches and blisters, that I sat down under a shade tree for our lunch break.

I had not sat there five minutes before I heard a bloodcurdling scream, followed by a long stream of obscenities. We all knew that someone was in trouble, and turned to see what would happen. "Some idiot hoed down a whole section of tomato plants and left the weeds!" the supervisor screamed. Like the others, I looked around, wondering what moron he could have been talking about. After questioning a few people, the supervisor discovered who had done it.

It was I!

I can honestly say that I was working in total sincerity—and working *hard*—trying to give my boss a full return for my wages. Instead, I had done more damage than good. Sincerity is certainly a wonderful thing, but this very embarrassing incident illustrates an important truth: You can be totally sincere but be sincerely wrong. This has direct application to the process of growing in grace.

I am reminded of this story when I hear Christians speak in glowing terms of the qualities of self-discipline and dedication. Those are qualities that we instinctively seem to admire in a person. But self-discipline and dedication *in and of themselves* are not necessarily good things. We need to ask, Are these qualities being directed *toward the proper goal?* A person may be sincerely disciplined and dedicated but be applying himself in the wrong direction, just as I did in the tomato patch. He can be directing these qualities to the attainment of a meaningless or even harmful end. The Nazis are an extreme example of such misdirected dedication. They were highly motivated and supremely self-controlled, but these qualities were dedicated toward evil ends. The same holds true of the Pharisees in Jesus' time. They were possibly the ultimate in religious dedication, yet Christ called them hypocrites, blind guides, whitewashed tombs, snakes, and a brood of vipers (Matthew 23:13,16,27,33). No doubt the Galatians were totally sincere in their efforts to perfect themselves through obedience to the law of Moses, but Paul had no words of praise for their dedication to self-improvement:

> You foolish Galatians! Who has bewitched you? Before your very eyes Jesus Christ was clearly portrayed as crucified. I would like to learn just one thing from you: Did you receive the Spirit by observing the law, or by believing what you heard? Are you so foolish? After beginning with the Spirit, *are you now trying to attain your goal by human effort?* (Galatians 3:1-3).

Paul would undoubtedly experience the same turmoil of spirit were he to come back and witness the state of Christianity today. Just like the Galatians, millions of Christians have trusted in Christ for their eternal destiny and entrance into heaven, but are trying to live out their Christian lives through dependence on self-effort. Having forgotten, or never learned, the truth that Jesus taught—"apart from Me you can do nothing"—they are applying tremendous energy and concentration to produce what only Christ can produce, with disastrous results. In the same way I worked with my hoe, they are working feverishly—enduring blisters, sweat, and tears—to produce what God does not want.

To see evidence of this, let's step back and get a wide-angle picture of Christian life in America today. When I hear people discussing our need for God to send a "revival," I usually respond, "God *did* send a revival and nobody seemed to notice." In the late 60's and early 70's a tremendous wave of evangelism swept our nation. Thousands upon thousands of people from all walks of life came to trust in Jesus Christ. I was a part of that generation of new believers. Through my ministry associations, I worked with thousands of them as they progressed in their spiritual journey, and I have seen some recurring patterns—unfortunately, not patterns of growing in grace, but signs of increasing desperation.

To me, the thing that most characterizes this generation of believers is the *continuous search for "something more."* It is a spiritual restlessness based on the belief that "real success and fulfillment in my Christian life is just around the corner. Through the next book, tape, or seminar I'll find it. Through the latest emphasis, through more dedicated service, or through a deeper commitment to follow Christ I'll find the secret that will blast my spiritual life into reality."

In spite of the fact that they began their Christian lives with a dramatic conversion, dedicated themselves to living for God, and sincerely drove themselves to achieve their spiritual goals, that generation of believers has burned out in huge proportions. Those who haven't yet given up are still running themselves ragged in a frantic search for "something more."

A telltale sign of the search is the prevalence of Christian fads. Every year, it seems, there is a new buzzword that is repeated endlessly in conversations. Each year there is something new that "good Christians do." As in a toy factory, a new "Christian hobbyhorse" rolls off the assembly line each year, and eager consumers stand in line to buy it.

Early in my Christian life it was personal evangelism. We witnessed to everything that walked, and a few things that didn't. A pastor friend of mine once remarked, "My people are so well-trained that they could lead a fencepost to the Lord! In fact, I think a few of them have done it." On street corners and airplanes, in bus stations and door-to-door, we were the most witnessing Christian generation in memory. Our philosophy was "Anytime you talk to anyone for more than 60 seconds, it's a divine appointment to share the gospel." We were told that witnessing was the secret to enjoying the totally fulfilled spiritual life. We tried it with all our strength, and found that it wasn't true.

Next it was "deep" Bible study. We studied prophecy of the end times, learned to exegete the Greek text, and explored word studies. But soon we discovered that even study of God's Word can become dry. One day I blurted out my frustration to a seminary professor: "If learning Greek will make you spiritual, how come the Greeks weren't spiritual? The Corinthian church was a total zoo, and they knew Greek without even going to seminary!" Twentieth-century Christians have received more biblical input and have more learning resources at their disposal than any group in history. But is there any evidence that we are living on a higher plane than our predecessors? I don't think so.

Thousands of believers chased after the gifts of the Holy Spirit. I often get calls on the radio in which I hear someone say, "I'm filled with the Holy Ghost and I speak in tongues, but my wife and I are getting a divorce." Spiritual gifts are no guarantee either.

Fads have come and gone. For a while everybody was talking about "body life." Later our problem was a need for "worship and praise." More recently we all needed to be involved in "accountability groups." People have tried Scripture memory, having an early morning "quiet time," and involvement in prayer chains. These days I keep hearing about "integrity in the workplace." Next year it will be something different. In my counseling office I have dealt with people who have been heavily involved in all these things, but whose lives are falling apart around them nonetheless.

When people search for an answer and find that nothing works, there is only one possible result: *disillusionment*. That word describes the emotional state of thousands of Christians I have met across America. They are disillusioned with the teaching they have received because they have found out that it doesn't work. They are disillusioned with the teachers and leaders they have followed because they are tired of being manipulated. They are simply disillusioned with the whole Christian life. Because they know of no answer to their disillusionment, thousands of them have resigned themselves to a substandard level of Christian living. "This is as good as it's going to get," they think. "I tried the Christian life, and it doesn't work."

That last statement is very revealing. "*It* doesn't work," people say. Right there you can see the root of the problem. The Christian life is not an "it"! *The Christian life is Christ*—a vital personal relationship with the One who laid down His life for you, so that He could give His life to you, so that He could live His life through you. "Christ . . . *is your life*," wrote Paul in Colossians 3:4. "For to me, *to live is Christ*," he declared in Philippians 1:21. *He* is what we have been missing in the midst of all our highly dedicated efforts!

This is not a new problem. The writers of the New Testament warn repeatedly against our tendency to stray from the real center of our lives—Jesus Christ Himself. Throughout his letters Paul expressed his deep concern that people stay firmly rooted to this one and only foundation:

> I am jealous for you with a godly jealousy. I promised you to one husband, to Christ, so that I might present you as a pure

virgin to Him. But I am afraid that just as Eve was deceived by the serpent's cunning, *your minds may somehow be led astray from your sincere and pure devotion to Christ* (2 Corinthians 11:2,3).

This can happen to any of us. We are all capable of taking our eyes off Jesus and focusing on the "wisdom of this world [which] is foolish in God's sight" (1 Corinthians 3:19). In the book of Revelation the Lord Jesus Christ addressed a group that fell into this trap. To the church in Ephesus, He said:

I know your *deeds, your hard work and your perseverance.* . . . You have persevered and have endured hardships for My name, and have not grown weary (Revelation 2:2,3).

This sounds so positive, but the Lord continued, "Yet I hold this against you: *You have forsaken your first love*" (verse 4). The Ephesians certainly performed good deeds, working hard and persevering in their man-made efforts. But they had obviously turned to the world for their wisdom and were motivated by their own accomplishments rather than by the love of God.

Like the Ephesians, we have often forgotten that Jesus Christ, who redeemed us in the first place, is alive and well, living in us, which is our only hope of glory (Colossians 1:27). "It is because of Him that you are in Christ Jesus, *who has become for us wisdom from God*—that is, our righteousness, holiness and redemption" (1 Corinthians 1:30).

In my opinion, many Christians look at their salvation in Jesus Christ in the same way a teenager viewed a wedding I was performing. With glassy eyes she exclaimed, "I want to get married!" Notice she did *not* say, "I want to *be* married"; merely, "I want to *get* married." In her youthful understanding, to "get married" meant to have her day in the sun, to be the center of attention, and to wear a beautiful gown. Taking this way of thinking to its logical conclusion, I can easily imagine her wedding. Right after the pronouncement of "husband and wife," she expels a huge sigh of relief, thanks the minister for conducting the ceremony, thanks the guests for coming, and then turns to her groom. Giving his hand a vigorous shake, she expresses her sincere thanks to him for saving her from singleness. Then she goes out the side door, gets into a taxi, and goes home. Her goal had been achieved: She *got* married!

We often look at receiving Christ as the *end* of something—escape from judgment and hell—rather than the *beginning* of a new relationship of growing intimacy with our loving Lord.

Now, obviously, escape from judgment is part of the gospel, but it is not the whole gospel. Jesus defined eternal life this way: "Now *this is eternal life: that they may know You, the only true God, and Jesus Christ*, whom You have sent" (John 17:3). Salvation is a *new relationship*, a *new birth*, a *new life!* This includes, to be sure, the end of an old life of alienation from God, but certainly there should be "life after birth"! Knowing Him is the essence of that new life. It is when we stray from a personal relationship with Him that we dry up and embark on a fruitless "search for something more."

The proof of our personal relationship is not only in *our* knowing *Him*, however. By definition, a relationship cannot be just one way. Just as important: Does *He* know *us?*

In John 2:23-25 the apostle stated that many people "trusted in His name. But Jesus would not entrust Himself to them, for He knew all men. He did not need man's testimony about man, for *He knew what was in a man*." Unfortunately, the Christian world has lost sight of this important truth as it has embraced the teachings of popular psychology. Christ is the One who created us, and He doesn't need the psychology profession to help Him figure us out. As our Creator, He knows every need of the human heart and has told us that all we need to know about ourselves has been revealed in the Word of God. The Christian is being duped into the incredible deception of psychology because we have either forgotten or never learned that Christ "knew what was in a man."

We read one Christian book after another explaining how to know *Him*, but we seldom read a book explaining how to walk by faith in the fact that He also knows *us*. We therefore end up saying, "God, I admit that You are more familiar with the things of heaven than I am. But You just don't understand what I am going through here in the 'real world.'"

The fact of the matter is that Christ *is* the "real world," and all the other things that we are enamored with will soon disappear. Remember: "Faith is being sure of what we hope for and certain of what we *do not see*" (Hebrews 11:1). In other words, "We live by faith, not by sight" (2 Corinthians 5:7). "So we fix our eyes not on what is seen, but on what is unseen. For what is seen is temporary, but what is unseen is eternal" (2 Corinthians 4:18).

Christ knows us, He understands us, He loves us, He accepts us, and He is the only true wisdom available to us. He is the solution to all our problems, and our peace in the storms of life. He, and He alone, has given us "everything we need for life and godliness" (2 Peter 1:3). He, and He alone, is the One who is "full of grace and truth" (John 1:14), and therefore the only one who can teach us "to say 'No' to ungodliness and worldly passions, and to live self-controlled, upright and godly lives in this present age, while we wait for the blessed hope—

the glorious appearing of our great God and Savior, Jesus Christ" (Titus 2:12,13).

A misunderstanding of this truth forces the Christian to become what the Bible calls a "double-minded man, unstable in all he does" (James 1:8). He *studies the Word to get to know God, but he studies the psychology books to get to know himself.*

Paul said, "For to me, to live is Christ . . ." (Philippians 1:21). In Galatians 2:20, he said, "I no longer live, but Christ lives in me." Since it is true that we no longer live, but Christ lives in us, let me ask you this question: If you want to get to know who you are, who are you going to have to get to know? *Him!* In other words, to discover *your* true identity, *you will have to discover Him who alone is your life.*

This eliminates the need for analysis, self-actualization, and going back into memories of past experiences to "understand yourself." When Paul said in Romans 7:15, "I do not know what I am doing," he didn't go on to say, "I therefore need to go for counseling." He merely recognized his condition of sin and death as revealed by God's law and claimed God's solution: "Thanks be to God—through Jesus Christ our Lord!" (Romans 7:25).

However, when we stray away from Christ as our life we have no alternative but to return to *self*-generated, *self*-centered, and *self*-disciplined religious experience, which is guaranteed to burn us out. That's when Christians are set up to seek after the "counsel of the ungodly," which the Scriptures warn against.

Every day I meet Christians who are painfully sincere—sincere as a heart attack—in their attempts to live the Christian life, but who are failing and feel barren and empty inside. They have tried rededication, the latest Christian fad, and deeper commitment to make the Christian life work, but have gotten no closer to fulfillment. Their shelves are filled with seminar notebooks, tape albums, and commentaries, and yet with all their increase in knowledge there is no increase in reality. There is no sense of fulfillment—only emptiness.

I have talked to many pastors who claim to have been "called to preach," but whose secret desire is to get out of the ministry. Ted had been in the ministry for several years, and seemed on the outside to be doing quite well. However, he shocked his congregation one day by resigning. As he explains today: "I knew the proper theology, and I knew the right things to say, but there was no reality in my heart. I finally got sick of continually talking about what I was not experiencing."

Leaving the ministry altogether, Ted got a job as a mortician's assistant. He had become cynical and disillusioned to the point that his job was a grim joke: "I figured that as long as I was going to be dealing with dead people, I might as well deal with dead people who can't talk back!"

Today Ted is back in the ministry and is an example of someone who burned out but later found the answer. Unfortunately, many others have not.

I can't tell you the number of Christian workers I've met who say they were "called to the mission field" but secretly hated every minute of it. In fact, if they were being totally honest, many of them would admit that they also hated God—at least the God they *thought* they were serving.

"We are saved to serve!" goes the cliché. "If you'll only get involved in service, you'll experience an abundant life." This is the promise commonly made to us, regardless of the fact that neither the Scriptures nor real-life experience will support it. Have you ever witnessed or been involved in a church split?

That is one of the most gut-wrenching and heartbreaking experiences I know of. Consider this: Who was in the middle of the conflict? I can confidently predict who it *wasn't*: It was not those "Easter lilies" who bloom (come to a church service) once a year. No, it was the most dedicated and hardworking members! Christian workers were right in the middle of the whole ugly mess. If Christian service will make you spiritual, how do you explain church splits?

In contrast to this backdrop of barren and loveless—but fervently working—Christians stands the offer of Jesus Christ:

> If anyone is thirsty, let him come to Me and drink. Whoever believes in Me, as the Scripture has said, streams of living water will flow from within him (John 7:37,38).

No, our primary calling is *not* to serve! The calling that is taught in the New Testament is *our calling to Him*. When we were lost, we heard the good news of how we could come to Him for eternal life. Now, as children of God, we can come to Him for love, acceptance, comfort, guidance, truth, meaning, purpose, or anything else our heart desires. After we *first* come to Him to receive and experience the abundance of life that He offers, He *sends* us to serve. Then, because we have first come to Him and are experiencing the flow of those "rivers of living water," that service is not drudgery. This is the same Jesus who said:

> Come to Me, all you who are weary and burdened, and I will give you rest. Take My yoke upon you and learn from Me, for I am gentle and humble in heart, and you will find rest for your souls. For My yoke is easy and My burden is light (Matthew 11:28-30).

In contrast to religions of the world which offer mankind "ten steps to spiritual fulfillment" or "the ninefold path to enlightenment," Jesus Christ continues to say, "Come to Me." He says:

I am the bread of life. He who comes to Me will never go hungry, and he who believes in Me will never be thirsty (John 6:35).

I am the light of the world. Whoever follows Me will never walk in darkness, but will have the light of life (John 8:12).

I am the gate; whoever enters through Me will be saved. He will come in and go out, and find pasture (John 10:9).

I am the good shepherd. The good shepherd lays down His life for the sheep. . . . I give them eternal life, and they shall never perish; no one can snatch them out of My hand. My Father, who has given them to Me, is greater than all; no one can snatch them out of My Father's hand. I and the Father are one (John 10:11,28-30).

I am the way and the truth and the life. No one comes to the Father except through Me (John 14:6).

I am the vine; you are the branches. If a man remains in Me and I in him, he will bear much fruit; apart from Me you can do nothing (John 15:5).

I am the resurrection and the life. He who believes in Me will live, even though he dies; and whoever lives and believes in Me will never die (John 11:25,26).

Jesus Christ did not just come to show us the way; He *is* the way. He did not just teach us some truth; He *is* the truth. He did not just leave us a manual to live by; He *is* our life.

Whatever the need of the human heart, Christ offers Himself as the solution. His eternal answer is *"I am . . ."*

When you were a small child and you scraped your knee or cut your finger, where did you go? Whose arms and comforting love did you desire above all else? If you are like most people, it was your mother. She would hold you, wipe away your tears, and then take you to the medicine cabinet to dress your wound.

Imagine how ludicrous it would be for some adult to witness a preschool child's accident and respond this way: "Here's a checklist of first-aid instructions. Go into the house, read the instructions, and dress your scrapes and cuts. You're on your own." Unless we're talking about a serious injury requiring immediate emergency care, any person with half a heart realizes that love and compassion is the child's deepest need, not a study course in self-help.

Much Christian teaching today reminds me of that heartless adult. Everything is "ten steps to spiritual maturity," "the five-minute Christian parent," or "six ways to overcome grief." It is as if the Bible were nothing more than an instruction manual, a positive-thinking guide to success in any area of life, with just enough religious talk to calm our consciences and quiet that still, small voice that keeps reminding us of our emptiness. In many ways we are just like the Jews of Jesus' day to whom He said:

> You diligently study the Scriptures because you think that by them you possess eternal life. These are the Scriptures that *testify about Me, yet you refuse to come to Me to have life* (John 5:39,40).

Rather than digging out of the Bible principles that we apply like a technician to repair our own lives, we are to go to the Word of God *to get to know the Person of Jesus Christ, the living Word!* Jesus said, "*Come to me*, all you who are weary and burdened, and I will give you rest" (Matthew 11:28). He invites every person to come to Him to experience His love and compassion, and to share His resurrected life. Just as the mother first gives of herself to her child before taking him to the medicine cabinet, Christ reveals Himself to the seeking believer, giving comfort and hope, before illuminating those areas that require the application of biblical truth that will set us free. I'm convinced that the devil doesn't care what our eyes are *on*, as long as they are *off* of Jesus. And that includes any one of a hundred good things, like Bible knowledge, fellowship, service, giving, or worship experiences. Anything we do that is not centered on the living Christ is a substitute for Christ. What God will bless as a supplement, He will curse as a substitute. The *good* is often the most deadly enemy of the *best*. The apostle Paul had all the background, experience, and credentials that religion had to offer, and yet this was his final assessment:

> But whatever was to my profit I now consider loss for the sake of Christ. What is more, I consider everything a loss compared to the surpassing greatness of knowing Christ Jesus my Lord, for whose sake I have lost all things. I consider them rubbish, that I may gain Christ (Philippians 3:7,8).

One evening I was listening to my wife as she counseled another woman over the phone. At "People to People" we are extremely careful to point out to people that we cannot help them, but can only introduce them to the One who can—Jesus Christ. Amy wanted to make that point clear to the woman on the line, and she shared an illustration that really caught my ear.

"No, we're not some kind of super Christians," she said. "We're just like a bunch of sheepdogs that are trying to herd the sheep back to the Shepherd."

That's it exactly, I thought, and I remembered what Paul wrote in 2 Corinthians 4:5: "For we do not preach ourselves, but Jesus Christ as Lord, and ourselves as your servants for Jesus' sake." So often we have made *ourselves* the message rather than Christ. No wonder we feel under pressure to fake it! No wonder we're wearing masks! But when we return to the biblical *message*—Jesus Christ, who laid down His life for us, so that He could give His life to us, so that He could live His life through us—we will see a restoration of biblical *power*. The One who said "I have come that they may have *life*, and have it to the full" (John 10:10) still transforms lives, just as He did in the first century. The problem is not with Him; *we* are the ones who have strayed.

Religion can never be more than a poor, pale, unfulfilling substitute for a personal relationship with the living Christ. God has made us and saved us in order that we may know Him and His love, and pass that same love on to people around us. In our sincere desire to grow in grace, and as we explore the many biblical truths that we need to know in the chapters ahead, we can never forget that we have been called, first and foremost, to a Person.

THREE

*Abiding
in Truth*

The pastor shook his head. "I understand what you're saying," he said. "I know I'm totally accepted in Christ. I know I'm a child of God. I know I'm totally forgiven in Him. And I know that the Bible talks about 'Christ in you.' But the whole idea of Christ living in me is just mystical to me. I can't get my arms around it."

The man who said this has been a friend of mine for many years. I had been invited to lead a small group Bible study that he attended, and I had explained what God taught me through my own spiritual pilgrimage—about how God had opened my eyes to understand more fully the truth of "Christ in you, the hope of glory" (Colossians 1:27). He was not disagreeing with the doctrine, nor being belligerent. In fact he has written a fine book emphasizing the Christian's total acceptance in Christ, and thousands of people have benefited from his ministry. However, in this candid conversation he expressed a frustration that I have heard from many other people who have heard the message of the indwelling life of Christ.

Is this message mystical? Is it a blind leap into the dark? Is it just emotional escapism flavored with intense religious belief? Or is it really biblical and realistic to speak of Christ living His life in and through you? And how does "Christ in you" relate to growing in grace?

Let's begin by looking closely at a passage that I have noted before. In it Jesus gives us the best illustration of the Christian life:

> I am the vine, you are the branches; he who abides in Me, and I in him, he bears much fruit; for apart from Me you can do nothing (John 15:5 NASB).

Jesus calls you and me the branches, and the desired outcome of the relationship between a vine and a branch is "much fruit." Let's think through the roles of both the vine and the branch. Whose job is it to produce fruit? Though any fruit produced will be *visibly attached to the branch*, it is clearly the *vine's* responsibility to do the *producing*. For example, if you cut a branch from the vine, how much fruit could come from it? Absolutely none! The power of production is not in the branch; only the vine can serve as the source of life and therefore fruit. The role of a branch is to be a "fruit-hanger." It can *bear* fruit if there is a vital link and flow of life between it and the vine, but its role is one of total dependency.

I have vivid memories of going on family vacations to the beach when I was young. My dad would go out into the water, stretch out limp, and float for long periods on his back. He could even take a nap out there. I would ask, "Dad, how do you do that?" His answer was, "Actually, Son, I'm not *doing* anything. I'm just relaxing out there." To me, it sure *looked* like Dad was doing the floating. But I discovered the truth when I tried it myself. The more I *tried* to float, the quicker I sank. That's when I discovered what Dad meant: My job was merely to surrender myself to the water. It was the water's job to hold me up.

This is the exact point that the Lord is making about the Christian life: *You and I cannot live it.* Just as a branch has no ability in itself to produce fruit and just as I had no ability to make myself float, neither do we have the ability to produce the life of Christ. The branch's "abiding" in the vine and my "surrender" to the water both illustrate our need to depend totally on Jesus Christ: "Apart from me you can do nothing." But how do we translate this "abiding" and "surrendering" into the kind of objective, intelligent faith that I have been describing?

I believe we will find the answer in another passage from the same Gospel. Speaking to people who had come to believe in Him, Jesus said:

> *If you abide in My word,* then you are truly disciples of Mine; and you shall know the truth, and the truth shall make you free.... If therefore the Son shall make you free, you shall be free indeed (John 8:31,32,36 NASB).

How can you learn to "abide" in Jesus Christ, who lived 2000 years ago in visible form, and lives in you today through the Holy Spirit? In these statements He points us to an objective and trustworthy standard of truth: "My word." Think through again the order of His teaching: First abide in His Word; then you will know the truth; then the truth will set you free. In other words the Son Himself, who is the truth, will set you free. I was once sharing these passages in a Bible study when a man wearing a confused expression raised his hand.

"I don't get it," Jack said. "On the one hand it says that we should abide in the Word. Then it says that the truth sets us free. Then it says that the Son sets us free. Which is it? Is it the truth, the Word, or Christ who frees us?"

I answered him, "Yes. All of the above." I laughed as he made another puzzled expression, and then I continued. "You see, Jack, there is no contradiction between Christ and the Scriptures. In fact, Jesus is the center of the entire Word of God. He is the *living Word*. Do you remember the first chapter of John? 'In the beginning was the Word, and the Word was with God, and *the Word was God*,' and '*the Word became flesh* and made his dwelling among us. We have seen his glory, the glory of the One and Only, who came from the Father, full of grace and truth' (John 1:1,14). So if we go to the Scriptures with humble, teachable hearts seeking to know the Person of Christ, that is where we will find Him revealing Himself to us. *To abide in His Word is to abide in Him.*"

The importance of not separating Christ as the living Word from the Bible as the written Word was driven home to me at a conference I once attended. A speaker got up and very fervently exhorted everyone to close his eyes and "think about Jesus." "Jesus . . . Jesus . . . Jesus," he whispered with emotion. I remember thinking to myself, "Suppose I *wanted* to think about Jesus. What would I think about?" Though I held back, I really wanted to address that question to the speaker.

What would he say? Was I supposed to visualize what Jesus *looked* like? How? No one on earth today knows what He looked like in His humanity. There are no physical descriptions in the Gospels, and no artistic depictions of Christ within hundreds of years of His earthly life. So to try to think about a picture of Jesus would be to focus on a product of my own imagination. As I continued to observe the way the speaker kept saying the name "Jesus," it seemed to me as if his main purpose was to induce an emotional experience in the audience. He was repeating the word, "Jesus," but there was no *content* to it.

Even though, as the popular song suggests, there may be "something about that name," the Christian's true knowledge of Jesus Christ is not based on a mental picture of His features, nor is "Jesus" a code word that should in itself evoke feelings of warmth and sentimentality, nor is His name a magic word that wards off evil and generates spiritual goosebumps. Christianity is an *objective* faith; that is, it is based on *facts—truths* upon which a person can *think* and *act*. To "think about Jesus" in a biblical sense means to meditate on a real Person—on the eternal Son of God who at a real point in time took on a human body and nature and lived among men, and whose personality and character is clearly presented in the four Gospels. This same Jesus later went voluntarily to a Roman cross to become a sin offering to reconcile men to a holy God. Then, having taken away men's sins once and for all, He rose from the dead and now gives that same resurrected spiritual life to any man, woman, boy, or girl who receives the free gift of salvation by faith in Him and His work. The same Jesus also promises a physical resurrection and a perfect eternity spent with a loving heavenly Father. These are facts that you *can* think about!

Christianity stands alone, separate from the world's religions, because of its unique combination of the astounding claims of the man Jesus of Nazareth and its pinpointing of those claims at a concrete place and time in history. For example, there have been many other religious teachers in history, such as Confucius, Buddha, and Muhammad, but none of these (nor any other man) ever claimed to be God and also convinced a significant number of followers that he actually was God.

Though people throughout the ages have believed in many different gods, these were known only through vague legends and myths. No one claimed to have personally known Zeus or Thor, for example. In the world's religions you either find a historical religious teacher who claimed to know a way to successful living but was a normal man nonetheless, or else you find fanciful stories of gods and other supernatural beings who lived no one knows where or when.

However, when you turn to the Bible you find a relentless presentation of objective, historical facts. Persons, places, and times are concrete. Caesar Augustus, "while Quirinius was governor of Syria" (Luke 2:2), ordered a census of the empire, "so Joseph also went up from the town of Nazareth in Galilee to Judea, to Bethlehem" (Luke 2:4). John the Baptist, the forerunner of Christ, began his ministry "in the fifteenth year of the reign of Tiberius Caesar" (Luke 3:1). Within a few weeks after Jesus' crucifixion, Peter was proclaiming in that very city of Jerusalem, "God has raised this Jesus to life, and *we are all witnesses of the fact*" (Acts 2:32). Throughout the following decades we see the message of Christ spreading like wildfire, fanned by the conviction that "we cannot help speaking about *what we have seen and heard*" (Acts 4:20). The most violent persecutor of Christians, Saul of Tarsus, is converted and later explains, "He appeared *to me* also" (1 Corinthians 15:7). With lightning speed, especially considering that this was a day without television, radio, or printing press, Christians are found throughout the Roman Empire. When the last remaining eyewitness writes his account he closes with "This is the disciple who testifies to these things and who wrote them down" (John 21:24).

Right in the middle of all this solid historical setting, as the cause and center of it all, is a man who claimed to be God!

These things are not the result of blind faith or some emotional leap. They are presented as facts that are either true or are not. For almost 20 centuries, millions of men and women have examined these claims, have come to the conclusion that Jesus Christ is indeed alive and that He is Lord, and have entered into a personal relationship with Him. This is the foundation of our faith. It is rational, intelligent, and open to investigation. This brings me back to my main point: If we want to discover the real meaning and experience of "Christ in you," we must learn to take this same objective, clear-thinking faith that forms the foundation of Christianity and bring it into our daily lives. *Only in this way will we ever grow in grace.* The Jesus who made those claims almost 2000 years ago is now glorified and exalted at the Father's right hand, and He is the same living Christ who lives in and through us today through the indwelling Holy Spirit.

During His earthly ministry Jesus Christ continually pointed people to the Scriptures, the *written* Word that testified about Him, the *living* Word. In His criticism of the Pharisees He said, "If you believed Moses, you would believe Me, for he wrote about Me" (John 5:46). When He walked with the two disciples on the way to Emmaus after His resurrection, He challenged their despondent attitudes and said that it resulted from their unbelief:

> He said to them, "How foolish you are, and how slow of heart to believe all that the prophets have spoken! Did not the Christ have to suffer these things and then enter his glory?" And beginning with Moses and all the Prophets, He explained to them what was said in all the Scriptures *concerning Himself* (Luke 24:25-27).

Later, after appearing to His disciples in His resurrected form, He said to them:

> "This is what I told you while I was still with you: Everything must be fulfilled that is *written about Me* in the Law of Moses, the Prophets and the Psalms." Then He opened their minds so they could understand the Scriptures (Luke 24:44,45).

It was necessary for Christ to open their minds, and to show them that the Scriptures, like history, are "His story." Today, He must open *our* minds before we can correctly understand the *meaning* of God's Word. First Corinthians 2:14 tells us, "The man without the Spirit does not accept the things that come from the Spirit of God, for they are foolishness to him, and he cannot understand them, because they are spiritually discerned." A true knowledge of Christ and His Word does not come through human intelligence, intellectual ability, or mere study. God says, "No eye has seen, no ear has heard, no mind has conceived what God has prepared for those who love Him" (1 Corinthians 2:9). How then can we discover the true knowledge of Christ? "God has revealed it to us by His Spirit" (1 Corinthians 2:10). That is exactly why you find so often in Paul's letters passages like this:

> For this reason, ever since I heard about your faith in the Lord Jesus and your love for all the saints, I have not stopped giving thanks for you, remembering you in my prayers. I keep asking that the God of our Lord Jesus Christ, the glorious Father, *may give you the Spirit of wisdom and revelation, so that you may know Him better.* I pray also that *the eyes of your heart may be enlightened* in order that you may know the hope to which He has called you, the riches of His glorious

inheritance in the saints, and His incomparably great power for us who believe (Ephesians 1:15-19).

Notice that wisdom and revelation are gifts from God, not learned attributes. Who does God give these gifts to? "God opposes the proud, but *gives grace to the humble*" (James 4:6). Recognition of who *Christ* is—God—and who *we* are—God's creation—demands a response of dependency from any intelligent, thinking person. However, our dependency on Christ is something of a paradox. On one hand, we need the written Word as our objective standard of truth; but on the other hand, we must live in dependence upon the Spirit of God to open our minds to a spiritual understanding beyond knowing mere words of ink on paper. God does not reveal truth *contrary to* His written Word, but neither does He want His people to become experts in His written Word whose goal is not to know the Person of Christ who is the living Word!

If we fall into the first error, that of seeking spiritual knowledge apart from the objective truth of the Scriptures, we are left defenseless and open to all kinds of mystical nonsense and error. We will find ourselves "tossed back and forth by the waves, and blown here and there by every wind of teaching and by the cunning and craftiness of men in their deceitful scheming" (Ephesians 4:14). Several times a week I receive calls on our radio program, "People to People," from listeners in this category. It is amazing to see the kinds of error that people can fall into who have no standard or plumbline of truth!

Larry called the program one night, seeking answers to his personal problems. Early in the conversation he said he was a Christian, but as we talked he showed an extremely weak understanding of the Word of God. I decided to quiz him more directly on his salvation. "Larry," I said. "Let's back up a bit. Have you ever personally received Jesus Christ as your Savior?"

"No, not really," Larry said. "But I did see His face in the moon once!"

In my counseling office I have heard Christians say some of the most incredible things. Now certainly any Christian can fall into a sin. That in itself is not a shocker. But I hardly know what to say when a Christian sits there calmly and tells me that "God has told him" to leave his wife for another woman. Can people really get that deceived? Absolutely! I've heard people justify unmarrieds living together, violations of trust, lying, stealing, gossip, and backstabbing—just to name a few things—without any qualm of conscience. How can they do this? Because they are ignorant of, or have deliberately closed their ears to, the objective standard of God's written Word.

I could tell many more stories. Some are more comical, like the woman who told me on the air that her "born-again experience" occurred the day she was sitting in her kitchen and saw a "cloud gathering and hovering beneath the ceiling." She claimed that this was a spiritual experience. Other stories of deception are very sad, such as the many families I have seen devastated by a member who was raised in the church, but was later conned into joining a cult. We simply have a desperate need for objective, unchanging truth to enable us to evaluate the feelings and thoughts that we have, and the philosophies and temptations that we encounter in daily living.

In order to worship the *true* Christ, we must be worshiping the *biblical* Christ! Any other Jesus is a figment of man's imagination, which can neither save you nor enable you to walk in the newness of His life. To "believe in" a nonbiblical Jesus is really just a form of idolatry—man's tendency to worship a god of his own creation. Only through the Scriptures can we learn absolute, authoritative truth about God, man, salvation, and life.

But we can get off on the other side just as easily. Mere words printed on a page, knowledge of doctrines, or systematic theologies cannot satisfy the "God-shaped vacuum" in our hearts that cries out for a personal encounter with the living God. Sincere, dedicated Christians can still fall into the same error as the Pharisees, to whom Jesus said:

> You diligently study the Scriptures because you think that by them you possess eternal life. *These are the Scriptures that testify about Me, yet you refuse to come to Me* to have life (John 5:39, 40).

John was a professor of Greek and New Testament in one of the better seminaries in America. He was a kind and gentle man, and his students and fellow faculty members liked him very much. However, inside he was not what he appeared to be on the outside. He was depressed, dried up, and increasingly desperate. Then one day he heard me talk about the living Christ on "People to People," and he came in contact at the same time with another ministry with the same emphasis. Finally he found the peace and joy he had been looking for.

"I always wanted to serve God since I was young," John explained. "It seemed that seminary was the highest echelon I could attain in Christian work, and Greek was the most challenging field. But of course once I got there I discovered the truth: My greatest need is for Jesus Christ Himself, and *you don't find Jesus Christ in Greek!* I had to become willing to lay aside all my education and knowledge, just like the apostle Paul did, to discover the 'surpassing greatness of knowing Christ

Jesus my Lord' (Philippians 3:8). I knew the Scriptures, but I was missing the living Christ *of* the Scriptures. You get to know Him only through humble, childlike faith."

How is it that a brilliant, hardworking scholar can study theology and be an expert in the original languages of the Bible, yet still miss Christ? The Bible says, "*God opposes the proud but gives grace to the humble*" (James 4:6). All of God's truth is addressed to the humble—to people who recognize their need for grace, that they cannot understand truth on their own, that they cannot live the Christian life on their own. Proud people cannot receive grace because they *will not* receive grace. They are convinced of their own sufficiency and enamored by their own ability. Therefore they can learn the words and debate the Scriptures but still miss Christ. You can very easily have a highly trained intellect but a cold heart.

According to my observations, there are few greater seducers of the hearts of God's people than intellectual pride. As Paul warned, "Knowledge puffs up" (1 Corinthians 8:1). But when someone like John has a responsive heart to the person of Christ, God will take that background of study, knowledge, and experience and use it in a marvelous way to build up the body of Christ. Today John has an effective and valuable ministry in counseling and teaching. Learning is certainly a wonderful thing, but in our study we need to keep the reminder of 1 Corinthians 13:2 before us: "If I have the gift of prophecy and can fathom all mysteries and all knowledge . . . but have not love, I am nothing."

In order to grow in grace we need both of these attitudes: a commitment to the Scriptures as God's revelation of truth for our lives, and a humble recognition of our dependency on the Spirit of God to empower us to know the God *of* the Scriptures.

In my life, a humble man I met almost 20 years ago named Wilber has stood as a reminder and motivator for me to continue studying God's Word with these proper attitudes.

I had only been a Christian about a year, and was still in the floor-covering business. I was attending an executive meeting in New York, which required a long limousine ride to the airport. After the dry and taxing business discussions I had been in with the high-powered environment, sitting in the back of a luxury limousine like a big shot had no appeal. I told the chauffeur, Wilber, that I'd rather sit up front with him.

After we chatted a while, I found that I liked Wilber very much, and wanted to bring up the issue of Christ. I asked him if he had ever heard the good news about Jesus Christ.

Wilber shot upright in his seat and asked excitedly, "Are you a Christian?"

"Yes," I answered, "Are you?"

"Yes, sir!" he said. "Boy, it's great to have a Christian riding with me. I don't get to meet too many folks who know Jesus around here."

The rest of that hour-long ride was sheer pleasure. After participating in all the superficial business hoopla, Wilber was a huge breath of fresh air. We talked about how we came to believe in Christ, about how knowing Him had changed our family lives, and of what we had learned about life in general. As we talked, it became obvious to me that Wilber was an extremely wise man. Through his years of enjoying an intimate relationship with Christ, the wisdom of God had come to permeate his being. My respect for him grew as the time passed.

Then the conversation took an unexpected turn. As I was talking about my experience in studying the Bible, Wilber mentioned that he didn't have one. "You don't own a Bible?" I asked, very surprised. "Well, I'd like to give you one, Wilber. Just give me your address, and as soon as I get back to the office I'll mail you one."

Wilber was hesitant, and he mumbled a little with a troubled look on his face. Then he said, "Mr. George, that would be nice of you, but it wouldn't be worth your time or money. I don't know how to read."

I was shocked. Here was a man with as solid a grasp on biblical truth as I had ever encountered, and yet he was saying that he didn't even have the ability to read the Bible. "Then how have you learned so much, Wilber?" I asked.

His big grin returned. "I may not be able to read, Mr. George, but I *listen real good!* I love Jesus, and so whenever I get a chance to learn some more about Him in church or on the radio, I perk up my ears and pray that God will teach me. And He always does."

When I got back home I sent Wilber something he could use—the New Testament on cassette tapes—and I have little doubt that he has used them to his full advantage. Regardless of his inability to read, Wilber has the most important qualities for growing in grace: a heart of love for God, an attitude of humble faith, and a teachable spirit. Most important of all, he has never forgotten that *his first love is a Person.* Upon those foundation stones the Lord Jesus Christ can construct a solid life. All a person with these attitudes needs is access to the truth of God, whether through reading or hearing.

My life has been permanently affected by Wilber's example. His hunger to learn has reminded me to take advantage of the reading ability that God has given me. But at the same time the wisdom that Wilber attained without formal education has reminded me not to become too enamored by my knowledge.

I've learned that if I go to the Bible seeking only knowledge, I'll get knowledge and nothing else. That's a great prescription for spiritual burnout! However, if my desire is to know Christ Himself, He will reveal Himself to me, and teach me whatever knowledge I need at the same time. That's a prescription for growing!

My pastor friend said that the message of "Christ in you" sounded mystical to him. In reality there is nothing mystical about Christ in you. It is a fact clearly stated in the Word of God:

> I have been crucified with Christ and I no longer live, but *Christ lives in me*. The life I live in the body, I live by faith in the Son of God, who loved me and gave Himself for me (Galatians 2:20).

Not only do the Scriptures declare the truth of "Christ in you, the hope of glory" (Colossians 1:27), but we are told as well that *"we have the mind of Christ"* (1 Corinthians 2:16). Where is that "mind of Christ"? In every born-again believer on the face of this earth. Therefore Christ in you is a true, objective fact that is meant to be experienced by every Christian. Because this is true, we as believers have a new source of power, wisdom, and knowledge, as well as everything we need for life and godliness in the Person of Christ who lives in us. That's what I saw in Wilber. From the outside you would describe him as full of wisdom, kindness, and common sense. But the real source of those qualities is Christ—alive, living in him, his only hope of glory. That is the foundation for growing in grace.

FOUR

~

A New Identity

When I first met J.E. he was a very angry man, and had been for many years. The Bible study I led that night had raised all kinds of questions in his mind, and he came up afterward to talk at length about them. "I asked Jesus to be my Savior when I was nine years old," he said. "But I've never heard teaching like you gave tonight. Nobody ever taught me that I am accepted by God, or that Christ lives in me."

"What *were* you taught?" I asked.

"Where I grew up," J.E. explained, "we heard all the time about how perfect Christ was, and about how we should learn to live like Him—and if we didn't, God would judge us. It didn't take me long—I'd say late in my teen years—to figure out that I was never going to cut it. So I gave up trying. I guess I've been living in guilt and running from God ever since. Off and on through the years I tried to go back to church, but I just got more guilt piled on top of me. I have sat under so many teachers who made me fearful that I was afraid to turn in any direction because God was going to get me. This is the first Bible study I've ever attended that gave me any hope."

J.E. was at this time 54 years old. This means that even though he had been born again through trusting Christ at a young age, *he had spent at least 35 years running away from God.* Needless to say, you cannot grow in grace when you live in the mindset that J.E. had!

Tragically, his experience is not that unusual. Thousands of people who sincerely responded to the gospel message they were taught spend years thrashing around trying to make it work, but without success. In fact, it is my opinion that the average Christian's flimsy understanding of his acceptance and identity in Christ is the major cause of the superficial Christianity that is all around us. A knowledge of the believer's identity in Christ is an essential foundation block of the Christian life. *It is impossible to grow in grace if you are still unsettled regarding your acceptance before God.* Thankfully, though, J.E. became one of the greatest examples of a dramatic turnaround that I have ever witnessed—not that he totally understood everything that first night. But he certainly perked up his ears and became teachable. For the first time, what he was hearing under the banner of the "gospel" really did sound like "good news." His hope was restored. And the key was discovering the unconditional love and acceptance of God and his identity in Christ.

"It's no wonder to me why you've been running, J.E.," I replied. "First of all, the Christian life is not trying to imitate Christ. What you discovered is the truth: You *can't* live it; only *Christ* can! You were taught to trust in Christ to take you to heaven, which is good. But that's not the whole story. Jesus Christ did not just come to get people out of hell and into heaven; He came to get *Himself* out of heaven and back into men! God did for you what you could never have done for yourself. He took away all your sins through Christ's death on the cross, then raised you to life spiritually. Now your role is to do the same thing as the apostle Paul: to reckon yourself as crucified with Christ, and to live by faith in the Son of God, who loved you and gave Himself for you.

"Secondly," I went on, "what you've experienced in running away from God all these years is the most predictable thing in the world if you don't understand His love and acceptance of you. You can never grow to know and love a God that you're too afraid to go near!" I went on to discuss with him the biblical truths which eventually set him free from the fear of God that had kept him in bondage for 35 long years.

The issue of identity is inescapable and central to our lives. "Who am I?" we all ask. "Where did I come from?" "Where am I going?" Tied up with this drive for identity are our needs for unconditional love and acceptance, and for meaning and purpose in life. Every human being wrestles with these questions and needs during his lifetime. These are basic spiritual needs, *and the answers we adopt determine the direction of our lives.*

"Identity" is often presented under the banner of "self-image." But as the apostles discuss our identity in Christ, it is immediately apparent that they are crossways with the prevailing philosophies of the world. Today, through the influence of psychology, the dominant belief is that most people have a "poor self-image," and that the solution is a "good self-image"; that they need to "love themselves more." Paul, on the other hand, says, "Do not think of yourself more highly than you ought, but rather think of yourself with sober judgment" (Romans 12:3).

According to God's Word, the problem of man is not a "poor self-image." Man's real problem is his overwhelming, egotistical pride! Pride was what caused Satan, originally a powerful and beautiful angel, to be cast from heaven. Pride was the root of Adam's decision to strike out on his own, introducing sin into the human race. Because that same pride is now in us, we puny people stick out our chests, thumb our noses at the Creator of the universe, and declare, "I'll do it my way!" That is why God gave His law to men: to humble their proud self-sufficiency so that they would be willing to receive the free gift of salvation through grace alone.

Therefore, having come to Christ, we do not need a "good self-image." *We need a proper self-image, an identity based on truth.* We need an image which not only has ourselves in correct perspective with God but also has us in proper perspective with other people. Here we discover a surprising truth: While we are warned against "thinking more highly of ourselves than we ought to think," we find that the identity given to us by the grace of God is more wonderful than we could ever have imagined—so great, in fact, that we need the enlightening power of the Holy Spirit to enable us to comprehend it! In its most concise form, my identity is this: I am a child of God, absolutely loved, and totally acceptable in His sight! That is simple to *say*, but that sentence has ramifications that we spend a lifetime working out and learning to understand.

Only through discovering and resting in our identity *as it is taught us in the Word of God* can we become free from the false identities that this world's system is always trying to put on us. The world is continually trying to induce us to accept an identity based on our appearance, abilities, family, or acceptance of others—anything but what God says. Our enemy, the devil, realizes that if he can influence us to depend upon any of these things for our self-image, then he can control us. Why? Because of this principle: *Whatever a man depends upon for his identity and meaning and purpose in life will control him.* Control comes through dependency. In other words, if I am dependent upon what you think of me for my self-image, then you will control me. If I am dependent upon my job for my meaning and purpose in life, then my job will control me. *It is only as we learn and rest in what the Word of God teaches us about our total acceptance before God that we can become free.* Only then we can go on to concentrate on the real focus of the Christian life: *knowing Christ.* And it is only as we learn and rest in what the Word of God teaches us about our total acceptance before God that we can go on *to love and accept other people* as they are. Our relationship to God carries over directly into our human relationships. We will ultimately treat others in exactly the same way we think God treats us.

Now let's look more closely at what the Word of God has to say about this identity we have received. Throughout the New Testament we find a particular phrase used to characterize our identity: *"in Christ."* In fact, this phrase or its equivalent ("in Him" or "in whom") can be found about 30 times in Paul's letter to the Ephesians alone! God uses the truth of "in Christ" to tell us that salvation is much more than an improvement or renovation project. As the Scriptures say, *"If anyone is in Christ, he is a new creation; the old has gone, the new has come!"* (2 Corinthians 5:17). It is important to keep in mind that we are *not* new creatures in Christ because of a change of *behavior* ("I used to drink, smoke, and chew, and now I don't"). *We are new creatures in Christ because we are in Christ and Christ is in us!* But to our twentieth-century ears this whole idea of being "in" someone sounds strange and elusive. A story I heard several years ago has provided me with one of the best illustrations I know to help us get a handle on this truth of being "in Christ."

Two boys grew up together. They were fast friends as children, but as they entered their teen years their paths began to diverge and they ended up in very different places.

Ernie was always in trouble. He began by shoplifting minor amounts of merchandise from stores, and worked his way up to stealing cars. Next it was armed robbery. Finally, on one of his capers, he killed a man. He was arrested, convicted, and sentenced to death.

Mike took a different track. He turned away from the rebellious tendencies of his friend and continued through school. He worked his way through college, graduated, and became a successful businessman. However, Mike had much difficulty with his physical health. His eyes in particular were weak. As he grew older, his eyesight deteriorated until he was legally blind.

One day Mike heard the news about his old friend Ernie. He felt a terrific compassion and sorrow for what had happened to his childhood friend, and he reached out to him. After writing letters to renew their old relationship, he went to visit Ernie in prison. They had a very touching and emotional reunion there, speaking by phone across the security window at the penitentiary.

In spite of years of hard-hearted living, something in Ernie warmed as he talked with the man with whom he had played as a boy so many years before. And an idea began to grow as well. Ernie was about to die; his friend was sightless. Was it possible that Ernie could do something worthwhile in his death? Could he give his eyes so that his old friend could see?

It turned out to be medically possible, and that is exactly what happened. Ernie was executed for his crime, but through surgery his good eyes were used to restore Mike's vision.

This story has always intrigued me—a murderer's eyes being transplanted into the body of a law-abiding citizen. What determines the identity of those eyes? Whose were they before? A murderer's. Whose are they *now?* Mike's. Imagine this scene: A friend of Mike comes up and says, "Hey, Mike, how are you? You're looking great ... except ... " He leans closer, squints, and exclaims in horror, "Do you realize that you have a *murderer's eyes?*"

"How stupid!" you would say, and you are right. The character or behavior of the person who looked through those eyes before is absolutely irrelevant now. They belong to Mike. Those eyes take on the identity of the person in whom they live.

Like the "murderer's eyes" that were transplanted into the body of another man, the Bible teaches that you and I have been "transplanted" into Jesus Christ! Romans 6:3,4 says:

> Don't you know that all of us who were baptized into Christ Jesus were baptized into His death? We were therefore buried with Him through baptism into death in order that, just as Christ was raised from the dead through the glory of the Father, we too may live a new life.

The word "baptized" means to be "immersed in" or "totally identified with" something. In salvation, this is *the act of the Holy Spirit where He totally identifies a person with Jesus Christ.* This *spiritual* baptism happens to *every* person who puts his faith in Christ, and *at the very moment he believes.* Therefore 1 Corinthians 12:13 says, "We were all baptized by one Spirit into one body—whether Jews or Greeks, slave or free—and we were all given the one Spirit to drink."

Just as the eyes of a murderer were transplanted into the body of another man and received a new identity, so guilty sinners are transplanted (baptized) into Christ and take on a new identity! It no longer matters what you *were*. As far as God is concerned, the "old you" is dead and gone. That is what Paul meant when he wrote that "all of us who were baptized into Christ Jesus were baptized into His death" (Romans 6:3). "I have been crucified with Christ," he wrote in Galatians 2:20. How can he say this? Because our old selves—previously identified as "in Adam"—have been considered executed through our identification with Christ at the cross. My identity was once Bob George "in Adam"—spiritually dead, alienated from the life of God, a guilty sinner, and liable to judgment. Where is that man today? Gone forever! Now I am Bob George *"in Christ"*—a child of God!

If you have trusted in Jesus Christ, this is also *your* identity. But seeing this is just the beginning. Let's look in detail at some of the *results* of our position in Christ.

In Christ we have total forgiveness. "In Him we have redemption through His blood, the forgiveness of sins, in accordance with the riches of God's grace" (Ephesians 1:7). I was teaching on this truth not long ago when Bill asked, "I know I asked Jesus to come into my life many years ago, but I'm still not sure about this issue of 'total forgiveness.' How can I be sure that *all* my sins are forgiven?"

I held a pen in one hand and a Bible in the other. "This pen," I explained, "represents forgiveness. My Bible represents Christ." Then I placed the pen within the open pages and closed the Bible. "Bill, where is the pen?" The answer was obvious. "In the Bible," he said. "If the pen represents forgiveness and the Bible represents Christ," I continued, "where is forgiveness?" "In Christ," was Bill's answer. "Can you have one without the other?" I pressed him. "No," he answered.

Then I stepped forward and handed the Bible to him. "Now I'm offering salvation to you as a free gift. What do you have to do in order to receive it?"

"Just receive the free gift," Bill answered.

"Right. And when you have received Christ, what else do you have? Forgiveness! Because forgiveness is *in Him*! That's why Ephesians 1:7 says, 'In Him we have . . . forgiveness of sins.'"

Unfortunately, forgiveness of sins has often been presented to people as a separate offer in itself, as if I had presented the pen as a separate offer apart from the Bible. That was Bill's problem. Too many times the gospel has been presented as "Come down the aisle and receive forgiveness of sins." Certainly that is *part* of the good news, but that is not *all* of the good news! Salvation is not like a vending machine, where I can get a little forgiveness here, a little holiness there, or a little "power" of some sort. The gospel message is an invitation to turn to the Person of Jesus Christ by faith! And when you have received *Him*, you have *everything*. How do I know I have forgiveness of sins? Because I know I am *in Him*, and the Bible promises, "In Him we have redemption through His blood, the forgiveness of sins."

Because of the weakness of much current teaching on our position in Christ, I continually meet Christians like J.E. who are certain that they will go to heaven one day, but who live in daily insecurity. Many would confidently declare that Christ lives in them, yet they doubt whether all their sins are forgiven—apparently never noticing the logical contradiction. Jesus Christ could never live in a person unless all of his sins were forgiven. He died for you so that He could live in you! His life in us is our assurance that we *have been made acceptable* and are *secure* in that salvation.

> You also were included in Christ when you heard the word of truth, the gospel of your salvation. Having believed, you were marked in Him with a seal, the promised *Holy Spirit, who is a deposit guaranteeing our inheritance* until the redemption of those who are God's possession—to the praise of His glory (Ephesians 1:13,14).

Christ's living in us through the Holy Spirit is our assurance that we have been saved. He is called in the above verse a "deposit" (like a "down payment" or "earnest money") *guaranteeing* our inheritance! (By the way, the "redemption" spoken of in this verse is referring to the resurrection of our *bodies*. We have already been redeemed *spiritually*.)

In Christ we have been given His righteousness. As wonderful as God's promises of forgiveness in Christ are, there is more! Christ not only took away our sins, but He added something to us: His righteousness. Second Corinthians 5:21 says it concisely:

> God made Him who had no sin to be sin for us, so that *in Him we might become the righteousness of God.*

God took your sins and mine and gave them to the sinless Christ. At the cross He received our punishment for us. I have found that most Christians generally grasp this idea, but that is only half the story. God then took the perfect righteousness of Christ and gave it to everyone who trusts in Him. This is what the biblical word "justification" means. To be justified means to be *declared totally righteous* by God.

Therefore how does God look at you? "All of you who were baptized into Christ have *clothed yourselves with Christ*" (Galatians 3:27). If God sees the perfect righteousness of Jesus Christ when He looks at me, I don't know how to improve on that! And yet we continue to try, rather than relying on the clear promises of God's Word. Hebrews 10:14 puts it this way: "By one sacrifice he has made *perfect forever* those who are being made holy."

"How can this be?" Dave asked one night on the radio. "I still commit sins all the time. How can God see me as perfect?"

I answered, "Because your acceptance is not based on what you are *doing*, but on the *perfection of Christ that has been put to your account*. It's like a bank account, Dave. If you had a rich uncle who decided to put a million dollars in your account, that money is yours. You wouldn't have to beg the teller to give you a little cash. All you'd have to do is to believe the bank statement with your name on it, and begin writing checks! Christ's righteousness has been given to you as a free gift."

And yet, because they are ignorant of the riches they have received in Christ, many Christians continue to live in spiritual poverty, begging God for what they already have!

In Christ we have total acceptance. Our acceptance in Christ is therefore twofold: It is the removal of our sins (forgiveness), and it is the addition of Christ's righteousness (justification). Though most Christians have at least heard of these terms, I have found that people tend to think of them as separate truths, like "options" on the "car" of salvation. Nothing could be further from the truth. The reason you and I have received the forgiveness of our sins and the righteous standing of Christ is because we are *in Him.* God wants to settle our minds regarding our acceptance before Him so we will be free to enjoy a relationship with our heavenly Father, and so we will be free to grow in grace.

In Christ we have become children of God. "To all who received Him, to those who believed in His name, He gave the right to become children of God—children born not of natural descent, nor of human decision or a husband's will, but born of God" (John 1:12,13). When Jesus spoke of or prayed to His Father, there was always a tone of deep intimacy. He taught that all who believed in Him would have the same type of intimate personal relationship with God. However, coming from our backgrounds of alienation from God, and because of the sin which still indwells us, this is often very hard for us to accept.

Because they do not know about (or perhaps simply don't believe) God's wonderful truths of our acceptance in Christ, many Christians are still acting like Adam and Eve—hiding from God. Remember, J.E. did this for over 35 years. Many people put on a tremendous act, wearing their "Christian fig leaves." This is when a person uses external rules and regulations to appear righteous because he is motivated by fear and desperately trying to cover up his own spiritual nakedness. He will work feverishly in religious activity in order to avoid meeting God one-on-one, in much the same way as a workaholic immerses himself in his business in order to avoid facing the difficulties and problems in his life. But God has good news for us: He accepts us in Christ, and He wants to draw us to Himself in a loving personal relationship.

> You did not receive a spirit that makes you a slave again to fear, but you received the Spirit of sonship. And by Him we

cry, "Abba, Father." The Spirit himself testifies with our spirit that we are God's children (Romans 8:15,16).

The word "Abba" is an intimate term of a little child for his father, similar to our English "Daddy." In fact you can hear it said by small children in Israel today. Jesus introduced a revolutionary truth when He taught that a man can relate to God on this level. Because of who He has made us, it is not presumptuous to speak to God from a heart of childlike faith; it is what He most desires. The more I meditate on this truth, the more I wonder: How can we *not* be drawn to a God who loves us in this way?

In Christ we have total access to the throne of grace. Under the Old Covenant worship system, the Israelite had to approach God's throne through the priests, and there were more levels still. Only priests of a particular family line could serve in the holy place, and only the high priest could represent the entire nation once a year inside the holy of holies. However, in Christ we can all approach God equally: "In Him and through faith in Him *we may approach God with freedom and confidence*" (Ephesians 3:12). The only High Priest we will ever need has completed His work, so now "we have confidence to enter the Most Holy Place by the blood of Jesus" (Hebrews 10:19).

Christ died for us then so He could live in us now. We have all rejoiced in the results of Christ's death for us. However, as wonderful as those results are, the cross was not an end in itself. Christ's death for us was God's way of "clearing the decks" for the divine action of raising us to life. What is a dead man's greatest need? Obviously, it is *life!* In my experience, I have found that most people would describe the problem of mankind as being "sinners in need of forgiveness." Now that is certainly true, but from God's point of view there is much more. When God looked at the world, He saw not only sinners in need of forgiveness but a world of *dead men in need of life.* That's why Ephesians 2:1 says, "As for you, you were dead in your transgressions and sins."

When God created Adam He said, "You must not eat from the tree of the knowledge of good and evil, for when you eat of it you will surely die" (Genesis 2:17). As we have already seen, Adam made the choice to declare his independence from God, and thereby introduced sin into the world. Having sinned, he died, because "the wages of sin is death" (Romans 6:23). His physical death occurred many years later, but he died spiritually that very day. From then on, having lost spiritual life, he and his descendents passed on their state of spiritual death to all men. Then God fulfilled His promises and did for men what they could never have done for themselves: "For as in Adam all die, so in Christ all will be made alive" (1 Corinthians 15:22).

> God, being rich in mercy, because of His great love with which He loved us, even when we were *dead* in our transgressions, *made us alive together with Christ* (by grace you have been saved), and raised us up with Him, and seated us with Him in the heavenly places, in Christ Jesus (Ephesians 2:4-6 NASB).

This is why Jesus said, "Unless one is born again, he cannot see the kingdom of God" (John 3:3 NASB). "The wages of sin is death" states a spiritual law; however, God has superseded that law with a greater law of grace: *"The gift of God is eternal life* in Christ Jesus our Lord" (Romans 6:23).

These truths are foundational for growing in grace. Apart from this understanding a person simply will not be able to make the Christian life come together. You can see this acted out during J.E.'s years of wandering, and you can also see why anger and fear were his daily experience. His bitter attitude toward "God and the church" spilled over into his relationships with other people. He tended to be an unfriendly, negative, self-centered loner. Frankly, J.E. was just not very pleasant to be around. Failed relationships dotted the landscape of his past, building up to the biggest blow of all: the day his wife of 23 years walked out on him.

If J.E. was bitter before, he was positively hostile now. He later explained, "My continual thought was, 'If you were married for 23 years and still didn't know someone, how are you ever going to find someone else that you would ever be able to trust?'" Fearful of rejection, he made certain that he first rejected others before they got too close. Full of anger, fear, and resentment, he turned to the heavy use of alcohol. "I was so angry with my former wife that I couldn't even stand to be in the same state with her. Even Texas wasn't big enough!"

This was J.E.'s condition when I met him for the first time. He could not love people because he could not love God. And he could not love God because he did not know about God's love for him: "We love because He first loved us" (1 John 4:19). But when J.E. did learn about God's love and acceptance and about the wonderful identity he possessed because of his identification with Christ, he went free. In fact, he became one of the most outstanding examples I have witnessed of the transforming power of understanding the love and acceptance of God.

Unless you have witnessed such a transformation, it is hard to believe that a man can be remade almost overnight. But it can happen, and it happened to J.E. The message of God's love and acceptance freed him from the burden of fear he had carried for so many years, and losing the fear removed his anger. J.E. became a soft, kindhearted, giving man who would soak up teaching on God's grace like a sponge, often with tears of joy in his eyes. He had experienced enough personal failure on his own to be ripe for the good news of Christ's free gift of acceptance and life. He told me one day, "I always figured before that God was big enough for Sunday, but I would handle things the rest of the week. Now I know I need Jesus to live through me all day every day." He laughed and said, "The gospel sure cuts against our pride and self-sufficiency, but Christ is the only source of power and peace."

Not long after experiencing the joy of understanding God's grace, J.E. was rocked to discover that he had lung cancer. But his faith was only strengthened as he depended more and more on the Lord who loved him through the various ordeals of fighting the disease. Unfortunately, as often happens, several "encouragers" seemed to come out of the woodwork, pushing forward all kinds of advice on "how to get healed." However, J.E. responded this way: "I've had all kinds of people get worked up about getting me healed. They want me to go to faith healers and such. I've had to tell them, 'Look, I've already received the greatest healing I could ever need—I've been born again. I am not all that enamored with this world. Jesus Christ is alive, and He lives in me! What more could I want here? And when He decides it's time for me to leave this world, I'll go to be with Him for eternity. What could be better than that? As far as my illness is concerned, I have found that God's grace is truly sufficient for anything we encounter in this life." Dozens of people who attended our Bible studies during the following two years could give personal testimonies of how they themselves were encouraged by J.E.'s upbeat attitude and faith, even while they were trying to build *him* up.

It became apparent that, apart from some spectacular miracle, J.E. would soon die. The divorce that he had gone through years before had left many bitter loose ends. As the love of Christ increasingly took hold in his heart, he found the old hatred toward his wife subsiding, but there was still no relationship between them. He had maintained a close relationship with his grown daughter, but she was deeply hurt by the division between her parents.

As his health declined, J.E. began to feel an increasing desire to be reconciled to his wife, and a growing conviction that he needed to make peace for his daughter's sake. But there were many remaining hurts and grievances that were hard to release. One night during a Bible study in which we looked at Christ's finished work on the cross on our behalf, these thoughts occurred to him: "If God has totally forgiven *me* for all that I have done, who am I to withhold forgiveness from my wife?" The grace of God was working in his heart. As the Scripture says, "Be kind and compassionate to one another, forgiving each other, *just as in Christ God forgave you*" (Ephesians 4:32). Those who *receive* grace are the ones who go on to *extend* grace to others.

Though they had not enjoyed a friendly conversation in years, J.E. reached out by inviting his wife to lunch. There he asked her forgiveness for the insensitivity, hostility, and selfishness that he had demonstrated in their home for so long. "I acted like a fool," he said. "Since I came to understand the love and grace of Jesus Christ, I have seen how wrong I was." The change in J.E. was so dramatic that his wife openly accepted his apology and became interested in learning more about the message of Christ. The God of peace made peace in that family. During the final months of his life, J.E. impacted many more people by openly sharing his gratitude to God for His love and grace. When he went to be with his Lord later that year, he was a man at peace with God, with people, and with himself.

In order to grow in grace, we must abide in Him who is "full of grace and truth" (John 1:14). J.E. lived for years in fear, anger, and bitterness. But he experienced a quick and dramatic turn-around when his eyes were opened to the wonderful identity that was his as a child of God. In his life we can see that the gospel—the "good news"—is truly "the power of God for the salvation of everyone who believes" (Romans 1:16). That power is unleashed wherever the love and grace of God, given to us without measure in Christ, is proclaimed in its purity.

FIVE

ॐ

Faith
Illustrated

During the writing of this book I had the unbelievable experience of becoming a grandfather for the first time. My daughter, Debbie, gave birth to a handsome baby boy. While Amy and I enjoyed getting acquainted with our new grandson, we naturally had many family conversations about pregnancy, childbirth, and babies. My son-in-law, John, is a physician, and through him I learned a lot of things I didn't know before. Through those talks I found myself becoming more and more fascinated with the development of a new life from the womb to birth.

In particular, the baby's growth inside his mother caught my attention. Here you have this baby totally surrounded by water. At any time after birth this would cause death by drowning. However, the baby is attached to his mother by a lifeline, the umbilical cord. Through this connection pass all the baby's oxygen and nourishment. Though this growing child will be a true individual—no one exactly like him has ever lived on earth—and though he does have relative freedom of movement and expression, his life is sustained only through the life of the mother.

There is a striking parallel between the baby's dependent relationship with its mother and our life of dependency on Christ.

Because of its dependent life, a baby in the womb could say, "For me, to live is Mom." In the same way, because of our life-line through the Holy Spirit, we can say, "For me, to live is Christ." Therefore the New Testament pattern is to consistently tell us first who we are, and then to exhort us to present ourselves to God in dependent faith. Our learning to walk in these truths does not happen overnight; it requires the ongoing teaching ministry of the Holy Spirit working in and through our lives.

Ron challenged me in a small group Bible study: "If all that is true, why don't I feel like a new creature? I haven't become perfect since I trusted Christ—I still blow it all the time!" With a suspicious look on his face, Ron leaned forward and said, "What's the catch?"

The whole group broke up laughing at his honesty. Usually the person in a group who asks the hard question is merely saying what most of the others are thinking silently. I said to him, "The 'catch,' Ron—if you want to call it that—is you are a new creature in Christ who is still living in the old body. This is what the Bible calls the 'flesh.' Until the day that Christ returns and we receive resurrected and glorified bodies, we still live in an alien environment called the 'world,' and we still have sin dwelling in us. What we need is to grow in grace! But it doesn't happen overnight; it's a *process* that takes a lifetime."

"Okay," Ron said. "Then what am I supposed to do now? What is my part in this process of 'growing in grace'?" To answer, I read what Paul wrote in Galatians 2:20:

I have been crucified with Christ and I no longer live, but *Christ lives in me.* The life I live in the body, *I live by faith in the Son of God*, who loved me and gave Himself for me.

As we saw earlier, "living by faith in the Son of God" means both seeking the Person who is the living Word and abiding in the truth of the written Word. In this chapter we want to begin putting legs to this truth. There are three qualities that we will highlight to help us get a handle on living out our faith. These are *dependency*, *objectivity*, and *availability*. Let's look at them in turn.

Living by faith is a life of total dependency. Like the baby in the womb of its mother, and like the branch which is abiding in the vine, our life in Christ is a totally dependent life. Man was created dependent from the beginning. The first man, Adam, was created "in the image of God" (Genesis 1:27) with a free will, a living spirit, and the ability to love and be loved by his Creator and other people. Through this dependent relationship, his every physical, soulish, and spiritual need was met by God. It was at this point of dependency that Satan launched his attack. When Adam and Eve believed the devil's lie and sinned, they brought spiritual and physical death to themselves and all their descendants. Their "declaration of independence" led them into total bondage to sin and death. Only in Jesus Christ is man able to be restored to the dependent relationship with his Creator—and thus life—that Adam lost so long ago.

But being born again is just the beginning. Not only has salvation come through Jesus Christ, but He has also shown us how to live a dependent life!

Hearing this, Ron asked again, "How can this be? Jesus Christ is God. How can He be a pattern for how we are to live? How can I live like God?"

"You're absolutely right, Ron," I said. "Jesus Christ has always been and always will be God: 'In Christ all the fullness of the Deity lives in bodily form' (Colossians 2:9). But even though Christ is truly God, when 'the Word became flesh and made his dwelling among us' (John 1:14), *He lived as the perfect man.* Jesus said, '*By myself I can do nothing*' (John 5:30). How could He say such a thing? Simply because, having become a man, He lived as a man—that is, as God intended a man to live: by total dependency. That's why you find Him making statements like this: 'I tell you the truth, *the Son can do nothing by himself*; he can do only what he sees his Father doing, because whatever the Father does the Son also does'" (John 5:19).

On the night before His death on the cross, Jesus told His disciples that He was leaving them, then added what must have been a mystifying statement: "But I tell you the truth: *It is for your good that I am going away*" (John 16:7). How could His departure possibly be good? He goes on in the second half of the verse to say, "Unless I go away, the Counselor will not come to you; but if I go, I will send him to you." While Jesus was on earth bodily His life served as an *external* example. However, following His death, resurrection, and ascension, He could come again with the Holy Spirit and live in believers, unlimited by time, place, or numbers. And more, He could establish a dynamic *internal* relationship with us whereby we can live in the same dependent relationship upon Him as He did upon the

Father! That is why Paul could write, "I no longer live, but Christ lives in me" (Galatians 2:20). The Jesus who said "By myself *I can do nothing*" is the same Christ who likened our relationship with Him to a vine and branch and said, "Apart from me *you can do nothing.*"

Once again Ron piped up: "But what does that mean, 'nothing'? People who don't believe in Christ do all kinds of things!" Ron was right again. From our human perspective, there are a lot of things that people can do apart from Christ. In my own experience, for example, I was extremely ethical in my business practices long before I came to know Him. There are many atheists, agnostics, and members of other religions who have refrained from smoking, drinking, and other external sins. Many unbelievers have been good wives, husbands, and parents. Non-Christians have been good citizens and paid their taxes, and many have lived lives of self-sacrifice for the good of mankind.

The "much fruit" that we bear through abiding in Christ has often been wrongly identified, leading many people off the track. An error here can easily lead to working oneself to the bone "for the cause of Christ,"—sincerely, but in error. For example, as a new Christian I held the common view that "bearing fruit" equals witnessing—leading people to Christ. Now of course leading people to Christ is an extremely important thing to do, but it is easy to slide into a train of reasoning like this: "Bearing fruit is witnessing. I am witnessing. Therefore I am bearing fruit." I personally found witnessing fairly simple, with my salesman's personality and background combined with sincere enthusiasm for Christ and concern for others. But as I got drawn into more "religious" conformity, I was able to continue the *activity of witnessing* long after my heart became cold toward God and people! I can assure you today that, while people were born again and received eternal life through my witness, the quality of my heart attitudes was certainly not what God was looking for.

No, mere actions can always be imitated. God wants us to experience His life! We can only experience the life of Christ through total dependency upon Him. This life, the "fruit of the Spirit," is described in Galatians 5:22,23: "Love, joy, peace, patience, kindness, goodness, faithfulness, gentleness and self-control." This is the quality of life which the Holy Spirit produces in us, and it is here that we really come to grips with the phrase "Apart from Me you can do nothing."

Let's take love, for our example, because the Bible gives us an authoritative and specific description of God's kind of love in 1 Corinthians 13:4-8:

> Love is patient, love is kind. It does not envy, it does not boast, it is not proud. It is not rude, it is not self-seeking, it is not easily angered, it keeps no record of wrongs. Love does not delight in evil but rejoices with the truth. It always protects, always trusts, always hopes, always perseveres. Love never fails.

Try a little test. Before each description of love, insert "I am." Read it now, and see how it lines up with your real lifestyle: "I am always patient. I am always kind. I never envy, I never boast, I am never proud. I am never rude, I am never self-seeking, I am never easily angered, I never keep records of wrongs. I never delight in evil, but always rejoice with the truth. I always protect, always trust, always hope, always persevere with people. My love never fails."

How did you do? I don't know about you, but I never get past the first sentence. God's Word, daily observation, and human history all concur that love as God defines it is a quality that human beings do not have naturally. Yes, we may be patient for a while; for example, we can grit our teeth and hold anger in. But God's standard of perfection would be a 100 percent, unblemished record of loving others this way for an entire lifetime—not just in actions, but in our inward attitudes and deepest thoughts as well! The only one who ever passed this exam was the Son of God.

It is because of our glaring inadequacy in this area of love that Jesus' convicting Sermon on the Mount is so effective. There He said:

> You have heard that it was said to the people long ago, "Do not murder, and anyone who murders will be subject to judgment." But I tell you that anyone who is angry with his brother will be subject to judgment. Again, anyone who says to his brother, "Raca" [a term of contempt similar to "idiot"], is answerable to the Sanhedrin. But anyone who says, "You fool!" will be in danger of the fire of hell (Matthew 5:21,22).

It doesn't take me more than an occasional experience like my temptation to "stuff that guy into his tailpipe" to hammer home to me that apart from Christ I can do nothing, especially as I focus on love as defined in 1 Corinthians 13. Part of the reason that people get deceived into thinking they can live the Christian life on their own is because they focus on external behaviors and religious observances rather than on God's perfect standard of love. In my experience, for example, I quit smoking years before I became a Christian. I just decided one day that it was a stupid habit, and so I quit. However, after over 20 years of being a Christian, I am still learning to love *my family and friends* through depending totally on Christ to produce it! *Much less* am I ready to declare my sufficiency to fulfill Jesus' commandment to "love your *enemies*"! (Matthew 5:44). If you have any doubts about a life of faith being exemplified by total dependency, I cannot recommend any greater proof than simply trying to love people with God's kind of love! Let's look now at another aspect of faith.

Living by faith is a life of objectivity. Faith has no value in a vacuum. It is either valid or foolish based on its *object*. I like to compare faith to swallowing. Someone could say, "Swallowing enables you to live," and that sounds right. Swallowing food *does* enable me to live. However, I could also swallow *poison* and *die*, using the same mechanism that I use to swallow food to live. So it isn't the *swallowing itself* that nourishes me; it is the *object* of my swallowing—food—that gives strength to my body!

For another example that shows the importance of faith's object, let's take flying. You are leaving on a vacation, and you have a ticket for passage on a major airline. Is it reasonable to take the flight? The facts tell us that flying is an extremely safe way to travel. Only a bare fraction of one percent of flights crash. We must admit that there is a certain leap of faith involved, because you have to take 100 percent of yourself on the plane. But is it *reasonable?* Even though your emotions may be a little jumpy about flying, based on the *facts* you would be making a reasonable decision of faith by entrusting yourself to the jet to take you to your destination. Few people would call that decision one of "blind faith" or an "irrational leap."

However, suppose I called you to come over and look at my "tremendous new invention." I take you into my backyard and proudly show you the "airplane" I have just built. There it is— a contraption made out of plywood, wires, old tires, and a lawnmower engine. Then I explain my plan to take it up for a test flight—to get a running start off a cliff, as a matter of fact—and I invite you to go along. When you hesitate, I ask with an offended tone, "What's the matter? Don't you trust me?" Your only honest and intelligent answer could be, "No, I don't trust you!"

Suppose I respond with this reasoning: "Your problem is that you don't have enough faith! You're a negative thinker. If you only had enough faith, it would work."

Listen—it doesn't matter how much faith you or I have; if we go off a cliff in my homemade "airplane," we will both hit the bottom together.

You can see from these two illustrations that the *amount* of faith is not the issue; the issue is *the trustworthiness of the object.* A person could get on a 727 with fear and trembling, but find himself landing a few hours later safe and sound. Another person could get in my homemade flying machine with absolute confidence and total faith, and yet come down like a rock as soon as we leave the cliff. The *object*, not the *amount*, of faith is the issue.

My friend Major Ian Thomas uses a crystal-clear illustration to make the same point. This is the way he tells it:

In the ministry which God has given me, I travel 40 or more weeks out of the year. Suppose a man came to me and asked, "How much does your wife travel with you?" I would answer, "Probably about 20 weeks a year." Suppose he asks again, "Do you mean you leave your wife alone over half the year?" I answer yes, and he asks, "Do you trust her?" I would say, "Of course! Implicitly." Now what if this man were to give a slow whistle and say, "Boy! You sure have a lot of faith!" How do you think I'd feel? I'll tell you: I'd feel like punching that man in the nose! It would not be a compliment to me to say that I "have a lot of faith." That's an insult to my wife! I don't have "a lot of faith"; I have a great wife! That's why I can trust her.

In the same way, the issue is not *how much* faith we have. In fact, I believe that to emphasize the *amount* of a man's faith is an insult to God. Rather, the issue is *the greatness of the God in whom we believe!* I don't have a "big faith"; I have a great God! As we showed earlier, *the object of the Christian's faith is the Lord Jesus Christ and His Word.* We live in total dependency upon the Person of the crucified and risen Christ, and we step out by faith in the objective truth of His written Word, trusting Him for the *ability* to do what He wills, and entrusting Him with the *results* of our actions. So a life of faith is exemplified by dependency and objectivity. Now we come to the third characteristic.

Living by faith is a life of availability. When I think of the quality of availability, I always remember one of our weeklong conferences, and the example given by a blind woman named Marda and her Seeing Eye dog, Zesty. All week long we had the privilege of watching them work together. It was fascinating to see Marda's skill at commanding the dog, and Zesty's responsiveness to her master. More than just responding, Zesty was alert to dangers that Marda couldn't see, such as obstacles that could have sent her tumbling, and would protect and lead Marda in amazing ways.

But the strange thing is that what I remember best is when Zesty did *nothing!* Each day as I prepared to teach the group, Marda would sit at her table and Zesty would lie down at her feet. Zesty would maintain that position for hours every day— sometimes sleeping, and sometimes looking around, but never leaving her post. Whenever we stopped for a break or meal, however, Zesty was instantly alert and on the job. All it took was for Marda to say quietly but clearly, "Zesty," and off they went.

That faithful dog has been a terrific example to me of the way I want to be responsive and available to the Lord. He wants us to know Him and love Him, and to trust Him in our daily lives just as we trusted Him for salvation. And He wants us to be *available* to Him. "What would He want us to do?" people ask. The answer is, "I don't know; it would be different for every person." Our role is to be *responsive and available*. The written Word of God contains a tremendous amount of direction for daily living that applies to everyone. It covers things such as our work life, family life, attitudes and philosophies, and many areas of decision-making. If we go into the Scriptures with a humble and teachable attitude, being responsive and available to God's leading, He will get us where He wants us. As I often say, "It's a lot easier to steer a moving car than a parked one! Get moving on what you already understand, and God will guide you as you walk, step-by-step."

With all of our "go-go" mentality, coming out of a sincere desire to "work for God," sometimes we need to be reminded again of Jesus' pattern. Certainly He was continuously active during the three years of ministry we read about in the Gospels, but those years of ministry were preceded by *30 years* in which He did *no* public ministry. And yet when He was baptized by John, His Father spoke from heaven, saying, "You are My Son, whom I love; *with You I am well pleased*" (Mark 1:11).

For 30 years Jesus healed no blind men, taught no multitudes, made no prophecies. He lived what seemed to be an ordinary life in an out-of-the-way country town. But every day He fulfilled the greatest commandments in the law:

"Love the Lord your God with all your heart and with all your soul and with all your strength and with all your mind"; and, "Love your neighbor as yourself" (Luke 10:27).

Every day Christ made Himself available to His Father's will, and it was the Father's will to keep Him living a common life in Nazareth until the proper time. According to many human eyes, Jesus didn't do much for those 30 years. However, God views things differently. Jesus was always available and responsive to His Father's command. With all our sincere but misguided tendencies to go blasting off to "work for God," and with our natural inclination to return to Galatianism, we would do well to remember Jesus' first 30 years of life on this earth and the Scripture which says, "Without faith it is impossible to please God" (Hebrews 11:6). For me, outside of the biblical examples, one of the best models of availability is still a faithful dog named Zesty.

Dependency, objectivity, and availability describe the attitudes that Paul had in mind when he wrote,

> Therefore I urge you, brothers, in view of God's mercy, to offer your bodies as living sacrifices, holy and pleasing to God—that is your spiritual act of worship (Romans 12:1).

The attempt to serve God apart from a heart of faith can only produce the kind of "self-discipline" that He rejects—a return to Galatianism. On the other hand, God is looking for men, women, boys, and girls who will say, "Lord Jesus, here I am. Thank You for dying for me, and for rising again. Apart from You I can do nothing, but I'm presenting myself to You for whatever You are pleased to do through me. I know I can trust You with the results, and to complete the work You began in me."

The decision to trust God in this way is the entrance to discovering real love and meaning and purpose in life. It is the exciting adventure of walking with a loving God through this life, getting to know Him in the process, and seeing Him use you in things that are of eternal value. The decision to present ourselves to Him by faith is our part in the process of growing in grace. God, then, produces the results.

Once we have made this decision to present ourselves to God as dependent and available children, how do we translate this into action by allowing Christ to live through us? I have a simple rule in Bible study: "When in doubt, keep reading."

SIX

❧✦❧

Feelings in Focus

In the late 1970's, when the Dallas Cowboys football team was frequently going to Super Bowls and was known as "America's Team," a friend gave me a couple of complimentary tickets to one of their big games. I was thrilled to have this opportunity, and my enthusiasm was only slightly dampened by discovering at my arrival that our seats were very high up behind the end zone.

As long as the action was in our end of the field, we could see just fine. From our angle we could see from sideline to sideline, and could watch the offense's plays develop and the defense's reactions. However, when the action was at the other end of the field, all we could see was a distant mass of humanity running around like ants. I couldn't tell if a play gained 15 yards or lost ten. It was because of this wide variation in perspectives that the actions of the spectators around me caught my attention.

It first happened during one of the times that the line of scrimmage was at the far end of the field. The Cowboys were on offense and were just about to snap the ball when an official whistled and threw his yellow penalty flag into the air. We all groaned. The Cowboys were close to a score, and a penalty would be costly. One of the referees announced on his microphone, "Illegal procedure, number 73 on the offense, moving before the snap." At that instant the entire section around me rose to their feet and yelled, "Boooooo . . ." at the top of their lungs. I heard individuals nearby calling that referee every name in the book. "He did *not* move before the snap!" they shouted angrily to one another. "That ref is crazy!"

I momentarily forgot about the game as I observed the fans. I also wanted the Cowboys to win, and I too was disappointed by the penalty. But what fascinated me about the fans' reaction was that *no one in my section could have had the slightest true knowledge of whether or not the penalty was valid.* From our angle and distance, we couldn't see! However, the fact that they couldn't really know whether the referee was right or wrong had no effect on those fans' emotions. They were madder than hornets.

My attention went back to the game until the same thing happened again, only this time from the opposite angle. The action was now in our end of the field, and the Redskins had the ball, moving toward a score. The quarterback faded back to pass, spotted a receiver moving well up the sideline, and fired a bullet right to him. The receiver danced a little, but was finally cornered and knocked out-of-bounds. He had slowed down and relaxed, being at least six feet out-of-bounds, when he was just pancaked by a Cowboy defensive back.

There was no hesitation on the part of the referees. Three of them simultaneously threw their flags at the obvious personal foul. It was not only an obvious infraction of the rules—a hit out-of-bounds after the whistle—but it bordered on being flagrant enough for the offender to be ejected from the game. Guess how the fans around me reacted this time—exactly the same way as the first! They screamed, booed, cursed the referees, and vehemently argued among themselves. "It was a bad call!" "Those refs are blind!" "They're always against the Cowboys!" "The officiating in this game stinks!" All this *in spite of the fact that the play took place right before their eyes and the referee was obviously right.* I wanted the Cowboys to win too, but the referee made the correct call. Considering the flagrancy of the foul and the danger of such illegal collisions on the field, the Cowboy probably should have been thrown out of the game and fined.

I've long since forgotten who won the game, but the behavior of the fans is vividly implanted in my memory. In the first instance, they had no knowledge one way or the other about the correctness of the call, yet they screamed like madmen. In the second instance, they denied clear evidence right before their eyes, and again worked themselves into a frenzy. Why? *Because they desperately wanted the Cowboys to win.* They wanted something so fervently that they were willing to close their eyes to the truth. Their attitude could be stated "Don't confuse me with facts! My mind is made up." We are all capable of falling into this attitude, and it can only be corrected by a sincere commitment to truth.

We have already commented on the *objectivity* of the Christian faith in previous chapters. We saw that the value of faith is found only in its object, and that the object of our faith is Jesus Christ and His Word as our source of truth. *Objective living means focusing on, relying on, and acting on truth.* Learning to walk objectively according to truth of God's Word is a necessary foundation for growing in grace.

On the other hand, in the behavior of those Cowboy fans you see expressed the exact opposite of objectivity. It is called *subjective thinking*. Subjective thinking takes place when our attitudes and actions are formed not by *truth* but by our *feelings*. "I want something" or "I feel something," so therefore it is true. If we allow ourselves to fall into this kind of thinking, we are capable of denying obvious truth standing right before our eyes, even if it is the clearly written Word of God. I have often heard people say, "If I could see a miracle like the ones Jesus did, then I would have more faith." That is not necessarily so. Seeing is not necessarily believing! There were many people who *did* see Jesus' miracles and yet rejected Him. Even His enemies did not deny His miracles. As a matter of fact, in the story of Jesus' raising Lazarus from the dead, you would think that raising the dead would be enough to persuade everyone to believe, but here is what the Pharisees said upon hearing the news:

> Here is this Man performing many miraculous signs. If we let Him go on like this, everyone will believe in Him, and then the Romans will come and take away both our place and our nation (John 11:47,48).

The Pharisees' problem was not lack of evidence, since they themselves admitted Jesus' works. The real issue was that they were more interested in maintaining their own position, status, and traditions than they were in coming to grips with truth— even with the Son of God displaying obvious power and authority right before their eyes. That is how determined people can be to deny the truth.

Continuously, on radio and in my counseling office, I encounter people who are living totally subjectively, people who have decided that their feelings are the standard for determining truth. Some are living in direct contradiction to the Scriptures, yet justify themselves and say that their actions are not wrong. Others claim to have knowledge of truth outside of God's Word. They have a feeling; they "just know" that God has spoken to them, in spite of the fact that their decisions leave a wake of hurt, disillusionment, and confusion behind them. To depend upon feelings is to have a foundation that will crumble under the strains and challenges of the world. We are set up for total deception, and therefore bondage, apart from a reliance on the objective truth that we find in the Word of God.

The thrust of the Bible is not toward feelings; it is toward our *minds*. The outstanding example is Romans 12:2. After urging us to present our bodies to God "as living sacrifices" in verse 1, Paul immediately addresses the issue of our thinking:

> Do not conform any longer to the pattern of this world, but *be transformed by the renewing of your mind*. Then you will be able to test and approve what God's will is—His good, pleasing and perfect will.

Notice that Paul *doesn't* say, "Be transformed by the renewing of your *emotions*." He says that our lives will be transformed by the renewing of our *minds*; his admonition is directed toward our *thinking*. This renewing is not something that just happens to you as you passively sit. *It is the decision to present our minds to the Spirit of God through the Scriptures* to allow Him to use truth to dispel error in our thinking, just as light dispels darkness. It is learning to look at God, ourselves, and all of life from God's perspective (truth) rather than from man's perspective (error).

Emotions are the most vivid aspect of our experience. When you are in the middle of intense feelings, they seem like ultimate reality. When feelings and facts do not agree, we do have the tendency to give feelings the deciding vote. However, in spite of this, the Bible is not directed toward our emotions but toward our thinking. In order for us to grow in the process of the renewing of our minds, it helps to understand how our emotions operate, what their proper role is as God intended them, and how truth can set us free from the bondage of subjective living.

Emotions are responders. They only respond to what you and I put into our minds. To put it another way, *you feel something because you think something.* Think of a time when you were feeling really angry. What were you thinking at the time? Nice, sweet thoughts? No, you were picturing an angry scene or situation in your mind. Again, think of a time when you felt jealousy. It was the same thing, wasn't it? You felt jealous because you were seeing or imagining a jealous situation. No one just walks down the street and out of the blue is suddenly overwhelmed by anger or jealousy without any stimulus. You don't "catch" a feeling as if it were a virus. You think first; then your emotions respond.

Notice that I said above "seeing *or imagining.*" That is the second point we must understand about feelings. Our emotions are stupid; that is to say, they have no intellect. *Emotions cannot tell the difference between fact and fantasy, or between past, present, or future.* Our feelings will predictably respond to whatever we put into our minds. I remember once going to a horror movie with my brother and sister. We went to the movie to have fun. We laughed and talked, bought popcorn and candy. I knew it was just a movie, but when I saw Frankenstein up on that screen, I was so frightened that I climbed right under the seat. I embarrassed my brother and sister to death. I don't know why. I was only 18 at the time. Plays, movies, and television programs have the capability of pulling all kinds of emotions out of us—from intense anger to teary-eyed sadness—*even though we know intellectually that it is only play-acting.* I've known people who have gone to scary movies and tried to remain calm by telling themselves, "It's only a movie . . . It's only a movie . . ." But it doesn't work. They may know that it's only a movie, but when they see a crazed killer with a big knife standing right in front of them their emotions respond accordingly.

We can do the same thing to our emotions through fantasy. Jeri was a young woman in her mid-thirties, who was having a serious problem with the fact that she was still single. Now there was certainly nothing wrong with her desire to be married. However, out of her loneliness Jeri began to indulge in fantasizing. She began to imagine her dream man—how he should look, talk, and act. She started to create scenes in her mind of the dates they would take together and the things they would talk about. Jeri's imaginary relationship became more and more detailed, and, since it was taking place totally in her mind, it was perfect. They never had the quarrels, misunderstandings, or difficulties adjusting to one another that you do with real people in the real world.

Finally Jeri's "dream lover" fantasy became so dominating that she began to act it out. After getting home from work she would cook her dinner, set a table for *two*, light a candle, and have an imaginary conversation with her imaginary date! It was at this point that she realized she needed help and came for counseling. This story demonstrates the influence of the human imagination, and how powerfully emotions allowed to run free can take over a mind that is not resting in truth. Excessive fantasizing is very dangerous because we can invent an imaginary world that the real world cannot compare to. It then becomes increasingly tempting to retreat there from the difficulties of life.

On a less dramatic scale, all of us have hurts in our background. I can remember bad things other kids did to me when I was small, and *get genuinely mad today*—and I'm over 50 years old! Those things may have actually happened over 50 years ago, but if I recreate them on the "movie screen" of my imagination, *my emotions don't know that they occurred 50 years ago.* As far as my feelings can tell, that mean kid is tormenting me *today,* and my emotions are responding accordingly.

Have you ever gone through an old family photo album? If you are like me, your emotions were spinning all over the place as people and places were recalled to your mind. All you had to do was pick up a single picture of Granny sitting on her porch, and a whole gamut of memories came flashing by. One picture can bring to mind whole summers full of sunsets, cut grass, ball games, lemonade, and an ugly but lovable dog. It might remind you of a broken arm, a childhood crush, a mean principal, or how much you hated arithmetic. You might see in your mind's eye a funeral, or remember the moment you heard the bad news about Joey. Once these things are brought to the surface, they are no longer just pictures. There are emotions attached to each and every picture—some good, some bad, in varying intensities. All these memories were already there in your mind; they just needed a stimulus—in this case, a photograph— to bring them to the forefront.

Therefore, by recalling events from your *past* you can stir your emotions to respond in the *present*. Through continually mulling over past hurts, resentments, disappointments, and injuries we can make ourselves absolutely unable to function today. Those things may have happened a long time ago, but our feelings cannot tell the difference.

In the same way, we can also project through imagination into the *future* and produce emotional responses today that are just as real as if those things were actually happening. I once received a frantic phone call from a woman named Nancy. She was nearly hysterical, barely able to talk through her sobs. It took real effort to get her to tell me what was wrong. Finally I got the story.

Nancy had been experiencing some aches and pains, so she had gone for a checkup. At the appointment the doctor told her she was experiencing some early signs of arthritis. "He told me it wasn't very serious at present," she sobbed, "but that there was a possibility it would lead to paralysis." She broke down again, bemoaning the progress of her condition in the coming years.

When I had the facts together, I said to her, "Okay, Nancy, let me see if I can recreate what you're thinking. You have been diagnosed as having some slight arthritis in your hands. This illness has progressed to the point that you can no longer type, which for a legal secretary is pretty serious. You've tried to keep working, but your limbs have shriveled and gnarled up, so the law firm has had no choice but to let you go. At your advanced age, with your limited skills, and now with your physical condition, you surely can't be trained to do any other worthwhile job. You're out of money, and so you have been turned out of your apartment. The outcome of all this, and what you see in your mind right now, is yourself: your crippled body dressed in rags, eating out of garbage cans, sleeping in alleys, and selling pencils on a downtown street to get a few cents for bread. Is that about it?"

There was a long silence on the other end of the phone. Then a quiet voice said, "How did you know?"

It's no wonder Nancy was a nervous wreck! After spending days creating and meditating on that terrible scenario, anyone would be at her wit's end. Her thoughts were not true, but her feelings didn't know that. Her emotions could not tell that those scenes were just imaginary projections of the future, so she was experiencing terrible fear. What is the answer? Jesus said that "the truth will set you free" (John 8:32). Therefore, Nancy would have to be transformed through the renewing of her mind by turning back to God's perspective, truth, in regard to her situation.

"Nancy," I said, "can you type today? Do you have a job today? Do you have money and an apartment today?" She answered yes to all these questions. "Then let's give thanks to the Lord today. He said, 'Give thanks in all circumstances, for this is God's will for you in Christ Jesus' (1 Thessalonians 5:18). I don't know what is in your future, but I do know that the same Jesus who is in you today is already there! He is the One who said, 'Do not worry about tomorrow, for tomorrow will worry about itself. Each day has enough trouble of its own' "(Matthew 6:34).

We talked awhile, then we prayed together. Nancy did give thanks to God for how He had always provided for her, for His love and grace, and for His faithfulness for taking care of her future. And she went free again, as she returned her mind to looking at life based on truth.

Incidently, more than ten years later, she is still typing away. But even if she had gotten seriously ill, the grace of God would have been there all the way to give her comfort; the Lord would have worked through His people to meet her needs; and God would have fulfilled His promise found in Romans 8:28: "We know that in all things God works for the good of those who love Him, who have been called according to His purpose." Learning how to lean on the Lord by faith during life's frightening or pressure times is an essential part of growing in grace.

In the midst of those difficult tests we learn that the same promise which sustained the apostle Paul through his "thorn-in-the-flesh" experience is available to us. The Lord said, "My grace is sufficient for you, for My power is made perfect in weakness" (2 Corinthians 12:9). However, that grace which is "sufficient for us" is only available in the *present*, and it is only available for *reality*. It is not available for our imaginary projections into the future. I don't know how many times I have fallen down in this way. I am fearing something that I'm sure is going to happen, and building it up terribly in my mind. Finally I cry out, "Lord, help!" It is as if the Lord answers, "Help with what?" "This terrible thing that is going to happen!" I reply. The Lord answers again, "Bob, you *don't know* what is going to happen. That's My territory. But I've promised you that when you get to the future, I'll be there, and My grace will be sufficient. Why don't you get back to reality in the present where you belong, and let Me take care of your tomorrow?" Then I get back to the present, and finally relax.

When we see how our emotions predictably respond to whatever we put into our minds, and how they are absolutely unable to discern the difference between fact and fantasy, we can see how critically important it is that we protect our minds. My father, who was not a Christian until just before his death, taught me this vital lesson when I was a teenager. We were sitting in our den reading one evening when Dad abruptly closed the book he was reading and put it down. I was surprised, because I knew that he was not far into the book. I asked him why.

"Because I've read far enough to see that this book is filthy, and I don't want any more," he replied calmly. Being a normal teenage boy, that made me *more* interested in the book. I said something like, "Well . . . so?"

Dad responded, "Let me ask you something, Bob. If we sat down at the dinner table, and someone set a plateful of garbage in front of you, would you eat it?"

"No, of course not," I answered.

"Neither would I," he said. "And neither will I eat garbage with my mind. That book is garbage, and I don't want any more of it."

Dad said none of this with pious self-righteousness; he discussed the issue in a matter-of-fact tone. It wasn't a matter of religious morals, since he wasn't a believer at the time. But he was speaking with wisdom, and I recognized it that day. And I have come years later to recognize how rare that insight is, even among Christians who have access to God's Word. Too few people seem to understand the importance of protecting their minds. As a result, people continue to live their lives subjectively—according to feelings—rather than objectively—according to truth.

As a matter of fact, a great deal of poor Christian preaching and teaching has actually *promoted* this situation. When I was a young believer there was a very popular song that went "Get all excited, go tell everybody that Jesus Christ is King!" It was a fast, high-energy song, and it did get you excited. However, it was terrible theologically. Nowhere will you find the Bible trying to jack up our emotions so that we will go out and live the Christian life. Feelings are the most unreliable things in the world. They go up and down like a yo-yo.

In those early years I had the same experience over and over: I would go to a stirring church service, with the orchestra playing, the choir singing, and an almost choreographed order of service. Finally the pastor would get up and emotionally carry out the preaching of God's Word. He would practically pound his Bible through the pulpit in his urgency, and I would be sincerely moved. "He's right," I would think to myself. "This time, I'm going to do it! I'm going to live for God 100 percent!" When the service closed I would march out, full of resolve. Then Amy and I would run into some friends, and they would suggest going out for lunch. We would talk in the car on the way to the restaurant, and I would feel the intensity waning. Hours later, after a heavy meal, light conversation, and time at home, I could hardly remember more than a sketch of the sermon. By Monday morning it was business as usual.

Why is it like this? Because emotions are only responders. As long as you are actually in that service, listening to and watching all that stimulating input, your emotions run high. However, as you go back out to ordinary life and the exciting surroundings are gone, your emotions come back to earth. They are simply not strong enough to carry you consistently.

There are thousands of Christians whose regular experience is just what I have described. They go to energizing church services and get sky-high, then come back down for a couple of days. So they have to go back for a midweek service to get up again. Then they come back to earth, only to start again on Sunday. It is a wildly inconsistent way to live, a draining roller-coaster ride, and a perfect recipe for burnout. And it is not how God designed us to live.

In subjective living, the order is *mind, emotions, actions*. In other words, the mind receives its programming from the world. Then emotions predictably respond to those thoughts in the mind, creating desires. Then those desires are acted out.

God's order is the opposite. Rather than mind-emotions-actions, the Word of God exhorts us to live in the order, *mind, actions, emotions.* We are to first present our minds to the Holy Spirit and in submission to the Scriptures as our source of truth. Then, rather than waiting around to "get excited" or to "feel like it," *we are to step out by faith in obedience to God's Word.* Then, finally, we will find our feelings responding to that step of faith.

There are very few things in the Word of God that I can honestly say I *feel* like doing when I first encounter them. For example, read the following Scriptures and ask yourself how many of them *you* would do if you were waiting around to "get excited" first: "Love your enemies and pray for those who persecute you" (Matthew 5:44); "Whoever wants to become great among you must be your servant, and whoever wants to be first must be your slave" (Matthew 20:26,27); " 'If your enemy is hungry, feed him; if he is thirsty, give him something to drink. In doing this, you will heap burning coals on his head.' Do not be overcome by evil, but overcome evil with good" (Romans 12:20,21); "Everyone must submit himself to the governing authorities. . . . Give everyone what you owe him: If you owe taxes, pay taxes" (Romans 13:1,7); "Do nothing out of selfish ambition or vain conceit, but in humility consider others better than yourselves" (Philippians 2:3); "If you suffer as a Christian, do not be ashamed, but praise God that you bear that name" (1 Peter 4:16).

There is nothing natural about a person responding in these ways. To the worldly observer, such a person is a total enigma. His thinking, values, and decisions seem to be upside-down, and yet he appears stable, consistent, and mature. He has begun to grow in grace, but if you were to ask him about it, he would probably be surprised. He is only conscious of walking in dependency upon the indwelling Christ; it is *Christ* who is producing the fruit that you see.

The writer of Hebrews complained about the continued immaturity of his readers by saying, "You need someone to teach you the elementary truths of God's word all over again. You need milk, not solid food!" (Hebrews 5:12). He then went on to describe the marks of spiritual maturity:

> But solid food is for the mature, who *by constant use have trained themselves* to distinguish good from evil (Hebrews 5:14).

Growth in grace comes to those who, through a totally dependent faith in Jesus Christ, *put the truth of God into practice.* It is the exact opposite of the philosophy of the world, which says, "If it feels good, do it."

Emotions in themselves are not bad. God did not create us to be emotionless robots, but rather to share His quality of life. It was the entrance of sin into the world that destroyed the harmony between mind, emotions, and will that Adam enjoyed. Now, until the Lord returns and we receive perfect resurrected bodies, we must be diligent to keep feelings in their proper place. They make a fine caboose on the train, but they make a terrible engine. Allowing our thinking, attitudes, and decisions to be dominated by feelings is to guarantee personal bondage and continued immaturity. Learning to live objectively—presenting our minds to be renewed by the truth of God's Word, and then stepping out by faith—is the road to experiencing freedom, and is at the heart of growing in grace.

SEVEN

Conflict Within

One of the most moving scenes I have ever witnessed occurred at the end of an annual weeklong conference for local leaders of "People to People" groups. There were about 30 people from all over the nation present as we enjoyed our final session together. As is our custom, we closed by allowing individuals to share what they had gotten out of the week of study and interaction. There were a few laughs, some tears of joy, and much to be thankful for.

Then we came around to a man named Gary. With great difficulty, through a voice broken with emotion, Gary shared that what he had begun to see most vividly was that he was a "wretched man." He quoted Romans 7:24, "What a wretched man I am! Who will rescue me from this body of death?" and said, "This is what God has been allowing me to see about myself. That apart from the Lord Jesus . . ." Gary couldn't finish his comment. He wept openly, but unashamedly, before us all. Many of us shed tears as well.

What made this scene so striking to me was that I would have pointed to Gary as an example of someone who had remarkably and dramatically grown in grace! To see what I mean, let me share about his background. He is someone who had to come from a long way "behind the pack"—at least outwardly—just to catch up to where most of us begin.

Gary had a lot to unlearn in his progress of growing in grace. His childhood home was a place racked with alcoholism, violence, and neglect. In an effort to find acceptance from people, he chose being tough and "crazy." By the age of 13, he was living on his own, sleeping wherever there was a space available, and had gotten his first tattoos. At 14 he played his first game of Russian roulette. As he says today, "Believe me, it was only to be accepted by the group I ran with! It was the only way I knew at the time to get respect from people." As he progressed through his teens, he would do things like forcing a needle and thread through his arm and tying it in a circle. Once he ran 15 safety pins at one time through his forearm—all in a desperate attempt to gain acceptance from people.

But while Gary seemed tough and crazy on the outside, inside he was full of fears and insecurity. "As a teenager, I had already determined that life was not all that great anyway, and I entertained thoughts of death frequently." It was natural that he would turn to alcohol and drugs for an escape. As usual, Gary went all the way, simultaneously using LSD, PCP, cocaine, and marijuana. "At this period of my life I figured out that I needed help, so I started reading the *Satanic Bible*, and got into transcendental meditation."

One night Gary and his roommate picked up two hitchhikers and struck up a friendship. They partied all night with drugs and rock music. In the morning the two travelers asked for a ride back to the highway. "On the way there," Gary explains, "I had the weirdest change of personality I had ever experienced. It was almost like everything I read in the *Satanic Bible* was coming to pass in me. I felt bigger than the car I was riding in. I felt like an animal wanting to kill." Gary and his roommate seriously assaulted their two guests and robbed them. They were caught, convicted, and sentenced to a minimum of five years in prison.

"One day in prison a preacher came in and talked to me about Jesus and what His death was all about," Gary says. "That night I committed my life to Jesus Christ. The feeling of being between a rock and a hard place lifted. Not only that, but the empty feeling I always had was gone. The next morning I was lying in bed thinking about what I had done, when another prisoner stubbed his toe and took the Lord's name in vain. Hearing that, I cried . . . real tears . . . for the first time in years. Soon I noticed that my vulgar language was gone. I knew beyond the shadow of a doubt that Christ Jesus was starting to clean out His home."

Gary, behind the walls of a prison, was indeed growing in grace. "I felt better after accepting Christ than I had ever felt in my whole life. I started seeing life for what it really is through the eyes of Christ. I started doing something toward people that I had learned not to do, which is *caring*. To others, prison life was the worst punishment that could be inflicted on them. But to me, it was like living in Beverly Hills. During those years I can honestly say that Jesus taught me how to live and walk by faith alone."

Finally paroled, Gary rejoined the outside world. "But the sad part is," he says, "that when the last gate slammed behind me, setting me free, I slammed the gate to my heart, locking Jesus in."

Gary seemed to be getting along fine for a while. But about a year after his release he found himself back in the drug scene again. His new marriage to Dawn had started well, but soon he found himself experiencing once again the "fussing, fighting, cursing, and hurting one another" of his old life. "I kept wondering why I had felt so close to the Lord and so free in prison, where outside I felt far from God and in bondage. I saw that our marriage was headed for an end in the near future."

He took a ride alone one night, and heard "People to People" for the first time. Gary's ears perked up to the message of God's love and total forgiveness. "Dawn and I started listening every night. John 8:32 became the verse that I continually thought about: 'You will know the truth, and the truth will set you free.' After much listening, it finally dawned on me that, even though I *felt* as if Christ were far away from me, He hadn't gone anywhere! One night I was thinking about these things in bed, and it was as if God gave me a snapshot of my own life: I could see myself walking out of the prison, and locking up Jesus in my heart. He was always in me, but I never let Him live through me. All those years He had spent more time 'locked up' than I had! I had 'committed' my life to Christ seven years before in prison. But that night I realized that surrender is something different. I had trusted Him for His death for me and His life in me. Now I needed to let Him live His life *through* me, because I couldn't do it. I got out of my bed, dropped to my knees, and set Jesus free to be God in my life."

To all outward appearances, Gary's life now reads like a success story. Yet this is the man who wept before everyone at the leadership conference because he was *now* discovering himself to be a "wretched man." How do you explain this?

Today there are widespread misconceptions of what it means to grow in grace. Most Christians, I believe, would expect spiritual growth to include an increasing awareness of one's own "holiness." They would predict that a person who is growing would become increasingly *less* aware of his sinfulness. Those views could not be more wrong. Regardless of the depth of our gratitude to Jesus Christ for all He has done, and in spite of all He has taught us in our spiritual pilgrimage, *we still have sin within us*, influencing us through thoughts, desires, and habits. We *never* grow to a point where we are incapable of sinning. As we grow in grace we actually become *more* aware of the evil within us, just as Gary honestly shared with our group.

Toward the end of his life the apostle Paul wrote, "Christ Jesus came into the world to save sinners—*of whom I am the worst*" (1 Timothy 1:15). It seems shocking to think of the apostle describing himself that way, and some would even call it false humility. But he was dead serious.

When we first come to Christ, most of us need no convincing that we have *committed sins*. However, we usually have little understanding of what it really means to be a *sinner by nature*. We have only begun to see our desperate need for a Savior—not only from the just punishment for our sins, but for One who would save us from *ourselves*. Over time He allows us to see more and more into our hearts. He progressively opens our eyes to see new areas where we have not yet learned to trust Him. He allows us to discover that our hearts really are wicked and deceitful when left to themselves. And He allows us to discover by experience the truth that apart from Him we really can do nothing. But none of this is meant to drive us to despair, nor for the purpose of condemning: "There is now no condemnation for those who are in Christ Jesus" (Romans 8:1). He shows us the truth about ourselves *so that we will learn to live dependently upon Him for the life that only He can live!*

The Lord's motive is to free us from the bondage of error, and to teach us to allow Him to live His life through us. Our failures do not shock or surprise Him. *He knows us far better than we know ourselves, and loves us still.* He takes us wherever we are, and works steadily and unfailingly to complete His work in us. We have to learn to say from the heart, "What a wretched man I am! Who will rescue me?" before we can ever rejoice with any depth in the answer: "Thanks be to God—through Jesus Christ our Lord!" (Romans 7:24,25).

This is why an understanding of the unconditional love and acceptance of God in Jesus Christ is absolutely essential for growing in grace. Apart from an assurance of His grace and acceptance, we could not bear up under this self-discovery. It is not always pleasant to learn the truth about ourselves, but the Lord's mercy is always there, giving us hope and reassuring us of His love. We can be thankful that we are abiding in a Person who is full of *grace* as well as *truth*!

There is a pattern of growth in believers—especially those who come to Christ as adults—that is so common as to be almost monotonous. When we are first born again, there is an incredible sense of peace and well-being. We have just gone from darkness to light, and believe me, we know the difference! There is a sort of "honeymoon period," where the Christian life seems easy. It *is* easy; we are Christ-conscious instead of self-conscious, and we discover new thoughts and habits becoming part of our lives without laboring. However, we also discover some other things. We find that there are still sins we can't seem to shake. Subtly, we become involved in the practice of religion. In the absence of reality—and in the fear of being discovered—we become actors, and the downward spiral begins. There is a waning of spiritual zeal, the loss of desire to read the Bible, maybe even a desire to drop out of Christian fellowship altogether. "It isn't working," we inwardly cry.

What has happened? Usually, a number of things: We have forgotten that our first love is a Person; we have strayed from Christ. We have not grown in the knowledge of our acceptance and identity in Him. Perhaps we don't know that He lives in us, and that the Christian life is lived by dependency upon Him. But along with these we have also picked up an erroneous idea of spiritual growth that fails to take into account the sin which still indwells us. That's why the common questions are: "If I am a new creature in Christ, why do I still sin? Why do I still have temptations? Why do I still fall into sins that I want to be free from?"

The Bible teaches, "If anyone is in Christ, he is a new creation" (2 Corinthians 5:17). But we need to understand not only what that does mean, but what it *doesn't* mean. In Christ the Christian has been raised up with Him to *new life*; he has been given a *new identity*; he has received the indwelling Holy Spirit, who renews his mind according to God's truth; his citizenship is now in heaven, and he has become an alien in this world; his spirit now cries "Abba, Father" as a beloved child of God. However, *even though he has become a new man spiritually, he still lives in the old man's body, indwelt by sin.* He still has the old man's thinking patterns, the old memories, and the old habits. He still lives in a world that stands diametrically opposed to the truth of God. He still tends to believe error until his mind has been renewed by truth from God's Word.

As we look in more detail at what the Bible says about indwelling sin, we encounter the biblical term "flesh." I want to clarify first that this word does not refer strictly to our *bodies*. God made us with a body. Our bodies are not evil in themselves, nor are they our enemies. It is *sin which indwells* our humanity that is the enemy. God created man as a spiritual being who lives in a physical body, but as we have seen, man chose to live independently of God. Therefore "flesh" is an appropriate term for the quality of existence of a person who is not allowing God to manifest His life in and through him. As a born-again child of God, the Spirit of God lives in me. The Bible describes an ongoing conflict between the Spirit and the flesh—between God's working in my life and my stubborn tendency to believe and practice error.

Here is how the apostle Paul describes the conflict in Galatians 5:17: "The sinful nature [flesh] desires what is contrary to the Spirit, and the Spirit what is contrary to the flesh. They are in conflict with each other, so that you do not do what you want." He went on to describe what indwelling sin produces:

> The acts of the sinful nature [flesh] are obvious: sexual immorality, impurity and debauchery; idolatry and witchcraft; hatred, discord, jealousy, fits of rage, selfish ambition, dissensions, factions and envy; drunkenness, orgies, and the like (Galatians 5:19-21).

Not very pretty, is it? Paul is not saying that every person will do each of these things to their fullest extent, but he *is* saying that these qualities accurately describe the nature of sin in man. The flesh can never produce the quality of life that Paul describes in the next verses, called "the fruit of the Spirit": Love, joy, peace, patience, kindness, goodness, faithfulness, gentleness and self-control (Galatians 5:22,23). These qualities are a description of God's nature and life, and no man can generate these on his own.

When you see what the Bible says about the nature of the flesh, you begin to realize that there is not a sin that you and I are not capable of committing under the right set of circumstances. One of the best observations I've heard was made by a good friend of mine named George. He grew up on an east Texas farm during the depression, and there is always a country flavor to his illustrations. George said one time during a Bible study, "You know, the flesh is just like a goat. It'll eat anything you feed it, like it, and come back for more!"

I think George hit it perfectly. I have seen discouraging tendencies in me just like that. In spite of the fact that Jesus Christ has died for me and given His life to me, and in spite of the fact that in my deepest desires I want to give myself fully to Him, I still find in me sinful desires and temptations that I know would only bring destruction and misery. Like Paul, I have found myself crying out, "What a wretched man I am!"

The truth regarding indwelling sin is rather strong medicine; it is not easy to take. Therefore it is good at this point to remember that truth is not always *pleasant* to hear, but *truth will set you free!* And one of the primary truths we must come to in our Christian lives is the truth about ourselves. *We will never be able to live the Christian life on our own.* Our flesh does not improve over time; in fact, it gets worse as it receives more programming from the world. How long will this conflict take place within us? *As long as we live in these unredeemed bodies.* You and I will not be free from the influence of sin in our flesh until the Lord Jesus returns and gives us new bodies to go with the new identities we have received—*but in the meantime we can grow in grace!*

When you come face-to-face with the reality of indwelling sin, you see the vital importance of the principle I shared in the first chapter: You grow in grace as you focus on *what God is doing* in the midst of what you are doing. To engage in prolonged self-analysis is not the answer. You'll find that a man is like an onion: You can peel off layer after layer endlessly, without ever finding a core. The more we try to analyze ourselves and discover "causes" for our sins and failures, the more we'll go around and around in circles, only to find ourselves deeper in despair. *The answer is not in ourselves; the answer is found in looking to our Savior and Lord Jesus Christ!*

One of the most concise biblical presentations of God's answer to the conflict is found in Galatians 5:16: *"Walk by the Spirit, and you will not carry out the desire of the flesh"* (NASB).

Notice first what this verse does *not* say. It does not say, "If you will clean up the flesh, you will become spiritual." You could work your whole life long and never get the flesh cleaned up. Yes, you could restrain your external behavior, but God is looking at your heart. Jesus said, "Out of the *heart* come evil thoughts, murder, adultery, sexual immorality, theft, false testimony, slander" (Matthew 15:19). Therefore it is an exercise in futility to dedicate oneself to "cleaning up the flesh" in the hopes of becoming spiritual. This is exactly what the Galatians were trying to do, and that is why Paul exclaimed, "Are you so foolish? After beginning with the Spirit, are you now trying to attain your goal by human effort?" (Galatians 3:3). Galatianism—that is, the attempt to attain spirituality through self-effort—is dedication to an impossible task.

It is imperative that we note the proper order in Galatians 5:16: If we will walk in dependency upon the Spirit of God, we will not fulfill or carry out the desires of the flesh. It doesn't say that the desires of the flesh will go away; it says we will not *fulfill* them. Even though in this world we will never be free from the *presence* of sin, we can genuinely grow in grace as we focus on what God is doing in the midst of what we are doing.

The apostle Paul had the same idea in mind when he wrote Romans 6:11-13:

> In the same way, count yourselves dead to sin but alive to God in Christ Jesus. Therefore do not let sin reign in your mortal body so that you obey its evil desires. Do not offer the parts of your body to sin, as instruments of wickedness, but rather *offer yourselves to God, as those who have been brought from death to life; and offer the parts of your body to him as instruments of righteousness.*

It reminds me of an AM/FM radio. I can have the switch on AM and listen to AM programming if I choose, or I can switch to FM and listen to FM programming. AM stations do not play on FM, nor do FM stations play on AM. I can't determine the programming that is being broadcast, but I can choose which one I will tune in.

In a similar way, a Christian can give his mind to the influences and philosophies of the world. His emotions and desires will predictably respond to that programming, and his actions will be characterized as the "works of the flesh." However, having been born again by the Holy Spirit, he can present himself to God for the "renewing of his mind" through the Word of God. Then he can choose to walk in that truth—that is, step out by dependent faith in God as his total sufficiency. He will then be walking by the Spirit. Galatians 5:16 gives us the promise that if we make the choice to present ourselves to the Spirit of God in this way, we cannot at the same time be fulfilling the sinful desires that are brought to our minds. *We will be growing in grace as we present our minds and bodies to the indwelling Christ, letting Him live out His life through us.* Immediately after exhorting us to "present ourselves to God as instruments of righteousness," Paul goes on to encourage us with this reminder: "For sin shall not be your master, because you are not under law, but under grace" (Romans 6:14).

When we face the truth that we can choose to walk in dependence on the Lord or walk independently, we can look at our reactions to circumstances in a new light. We now see that circumstances do not *cause* our spirit; they only *reveal* it. External events do not put sin *into* me; they draw fleshly reactions *out of* me. Therefore God often uses circumstances of life to show us where we are walking at a point in time, and as reminders to return to dependency upon Him.

Our family once had a dog named Peppy. If he weren't the stupidest animal God ever created, he certainly tied a number of records. One day during a terrific hailstorm I looked out the back window and saw Peppy standing right in the middle of the yard and just getting hammered by hail. Griping and muttering to myself, I ran out the door, grabbed the dog, and carried him through the house to the front porch, where there was an overhang. "He can stay safely here," I thought to myself. But no. Peppy ran out into the *front* yard to get peppered to death by hail!

Amy was watching all this through a window. In her matter-of-fact, practical voice she said to me, "What did you do that for?"

I was in no mood for a discussion. I gave her a look that would kill, and spat, "Aww, *shut up!*"

That was a natural and quick response, and immediately I felt odd. I couldn't remember having spoken to Amy in that tone of voice since before I became a Christian. Almost as quickly I said to her, "I'm sorry, Honey. I didn't mean to talk to you like that."

Amy just smiled and responded, "That's okay. You just got your nature revealed."

After saving the dog one more time and tying him securely, I went back into the house, where Amy, the kids, and I had a wonderful discussion about how in Christ we don't have to be phonies. As long as we live in this world, sin lives in us and is capable of coming to the surface, but that is not who we are. We are beloved, forgiven, acceptable children of God. And when we do blow it, we have the freedom to turn back to truth and walk in dependency upon the Spirit of God who indwells us.

Unfortunately, though, I have found that many Christians have expectations regarding spiritual growth and the nature of indwelling sin that are the *exact opposite* of the truth. In my opinion, these misconceptions not only keep them in bondage to failure, but they actually set people up for a greater and more guaranteed fall. One of these wrong assumptions is the notion that a Christian's flesh improves and becomes less sinful over time. This is a tremendous and dangerous error, and will effectively prevent a person from growing in grace.

You have to remember something about error: It doesn't have to be clearly defined in one's mind in order to cause damage. Many times the most dangerous errors are those that sit quietly in the back of our minds, but at the same time form *expectations* that mold our thinking and actions. They can be ideas that we have never actually thought through logically. The errors regarding spiritual growth are usually of this type.

While no one would *say* he thinks this way, there is a particular mindset that many Christians hold. It goes something like this: "At the time I was born again, I obviously had no 'Christian maturity' (or character), so I needed 100 percent of Jesus. Later, as I 'grew in character,' I became about 20 percent mature, so then I needed about 80 percent of Jesus. At some point, if I keep growing, I'll be about 65 percent mature; then I'll need 35 percent of Jesus."

I know no one who would have the audacity to make the following comment out loud, but it is the *logical conclusion* of that kind of thinking: "Someday I'll have achieved such a level of Christian character—100 percent mature—that *I won't need Jesus at all.*"

Alongside this belief in the "growth of Christian character" comes the corresponding thought that the flesh is becoming less sinful. *Therefore,* the person believes, *I am less temptable to sin.* I can't think of a more dangerous situation than to be going through life thinking you are becoming immune to temptation. I guarantee that if you believe this you are being set up for a serious fall!

People ask me, "Where do you see evidence of this?" There are many situations where this hidden expectation shows through. I usually see the most vivid examples in my counseling office: the dozens of times a man or woman has sat slumped in a chair, mouth agape and eyes wide in disbelief, saying, "I've been a Christian for 15 years, and *I can't believe what I just did,*" or, "I can't believe I'm wrestling with this temptation." The same thoughts can be seen in Christians' response to other believers' sins. Some well-known Christian falls, or a pastor is revealed to have given in to temptation, and people say, "He was a man of

God. He's taught the Bible wonderfully and led many people to Christ. I can't believe he did this."

What do those comments reveal? The expectation that a Christian who has shown marks of maturity and of being used by God (and I am not doubting either) somehow gets to a state where he is not capable of responding to the same sinful desires that are common to man. We simply will not accept the biblical teaching that, as Paul said, *"Nothing good dwells in me, that is, in my flesh"* (Romans 7:18 NASB). No, we tend to believe that our need for Christ is like the old hair cream slogan: "A little dab'l do ya."

Christians who believe that they are less temptable or that they have achieved some kind of permanent victory over sin tend to take foolish chances. They play with fire, thinking that they cannot be burned. These are the ones who find themselves blindsided by a sudden temptation, and end up in a counseling office saying, "I can't believe what I did." If they had understood the evil in their own flesh from the start, they would have known not to play around with potential trouble, and could have avoided a great deal of personal misery.

The hard truth is this: The sin in our flesh was absolutely rotten the day we came to Christ, and after 50 years it will still be rotten. Jesus' words will never change: "Apart from Me you can do nothing." Therefore our need for total dependency upon Christ was 100 percent the first day, 100 percent after 50 years, and—even if we walk faithfully with the Lord for a full century—our need for total dependency upon the living Christ will still be 100 percent!

The Bible teaches that we are engaged in spiritual warfare: "For our struggle is not against flesh and blood, but against the rulers, against the authorities, against the powers of this dark world and against the spiritual forces of evil in the heavenly realms" (Ephesians 6:12). Though most Christians would readily agree to this statement, I find that many are confused as to the nature of the conflict.

When you say the words "spiritual warfare," it is common for people to visualize *Exorcist*-type encounters of demonic possession and the like. While I admit these as a biblical possibility, they are certainly not the *norm*. In my opinion *the real issue in spiritual warfare is truth versus error, and the battleground is the minds of men.* As Jesus said,

> If you hold to My teaching, you are really My disciples. Then you will know the truth, and the truth will set you free (John 8:31,32).

If it is truth that sets us free, then it must be error that binds us. That is why the devil's primary attack to frustrate the spread of the gospel is to keep Christians living in bondage through error. In speaking with Christians of all backgrounds, denominations, and geographical areas each night on live radio, I have a unique chance to get a bird's-eye view of what Christians are thinking. One clear observation I have made is the prevalence of *fear*. People are full of fear about their personal problems, about their marriages, about how their children will turn out, about their job security, about world events. And tragically many Christians—though they have become reconciled, redeemed, justified, holy children of God—still live in abject fear of God.

I am convinced that Satan's primary weapon against the Christian is fear. I often tell people, "Satan is a toothless wonder. You don't have to be afraid of the devil. He may be a 'roaring lion looking for someone to devour' (1 Peter 5:8), but he has been detoothed and declawed at the cross! 'Greater is He who is in you than he who is in the world' (1 John 4:4 NASB). The devil cannot hurt us, but he *can* lie, deceive, and try to frighten us." This is an effective attack because people who are motivated by deep fear tend to do very foolish things. They do not think clearly, nor do they act wisely. You lose perspective when you are afraid.

The devil's lies are particularly effective when they are aimed at our *identity*. Let's say that we have stolen something. Satan is not satisfied when we commit the theft. He tries to infect our minds with the thought, "You are a thief." It is not enough for us simply to admit having told a lie. The devil whispers, "You are a liar." He is not satisfied that we admit committing a sin. He wants us to think, "I am a sinner." The *last* thing that Satan wants is for a Christian to think, "I am a child of God who has committed a sin." Why? Because the very next step would be, "That makes no sense! If I am a saint, a holy one of God, then that behavior is entirely inconsistent with who I really am." A believer who sees himself this way, which is the way God sees him, will get up, return to dependency on Christ, and go on with his life. But if he really buys the idea, "I am a sinner," then sinning is accepted as natural. After all, the only behavior you can expect from a sinner is sin. The person who thinks this way will eventually lose hope and give up. Then Satan will bring in the idea that "God is holy, and hates sin." For the person whose identity is "sinner," abject fear of God can be the only result.

That is why the love and acceptance of God is not only the foundation of our Christian lives, it is the center around which we must orbit as we grow in grace. Grace is not only how we were *saved*, it is how we *live*.

Another place where you see people's erroneous beliefs in their understanding of their own sinful nature is in their judgmental attitudes toward others. I went to get dressed after finishing a workout one day, only to walk into one of those situations I dread. Some "locker room preacher" was holding court. He grew louder and louder and gestured enthusiastically as he cowed three increasingly embarrassed companions into submission. I was trying to ignore the scene, but to no avail. Then I began to pick up the subject of his tirade, and my blood began to boil. He was talking about a man I knew, who happened to be a professor at a nearby Bible college where this "preacher" was a student.

"There is no way that (he named the man) is a Christian!" he declared. "I happen to know that he is a homosexual. The Bible says, 'Do not be deceived: Neither the sexually immoral nor idolaters nor adulterers nor male prostitutes nor homosexual offenders . . . will inherit the kingdom of God'—1 Corinthians 6:9,10."

I was really angry now and wondering what to do, when the preacher noticed me. He turned to me, certain that I would support his position, and said, "What do you think about that, Mr. George?"

"I'll tell you what I think," I said in measured tones. "I think you failed to quote the whole verse. Also in that lineup are 'thieves,' 'greedy,' 'drunkards,' 'slanderers,' and 'swindlers.'" I moved closer and looked him right in the eye. "Now I have stood here and heard you publicly slander a man I know and respect. You are a slanderer. *By your own theology, you won't get into the kingdom of God either!*"

On another occasion I had an encounter with an older woman who was a well-known Bible teacher. She was giving me a hard time regarding my teaching on the grace of God because she feared that it would lead people to be "light on sin." "Don't tell me," she declared, "that if a man keeps on committing adultery, he is still forgiven! The Bible says that a person who lives in persistent sin is not saved."

I happened to know this lady pretty well. I asked her, "How long have you been a Christian?"

"Almost 50 years," she answered.

"How long have you had trouble with a critical spirit?" I asked.

She hesitated and got a sour look on her face. Finally she mumbled, "Fifty years."

I responded, "Now I'd call that pretty persistent sinning!"

You can see how in both of these stories the person's theology does not match up with real life. Both of them rely on a very selective view of sins in order to maintain their point. The Bible student was willing to consider homosexuality as a sin that no Christian could commit while ignoring his own sin of slander, even though they are both in the same biblical list. The lady would focus on several "really bad" external sins that "other people" commit while ignoring her own well-entrenched attitude sins. Both views lead to spiritual pride, blindness to the reality of one's own sins, and a judgmental attitude toward others. How different both these individuals were from the humility of my friend Gary, who discovered that he was a "wretched man!"

The fact that Christians can fall into various sins should not be that big of a surprise to us. And when they do, recognizing the weakness of our own flesh (that apart from Christ we are capable of falling into the same kind of trap) should cause us to respond to them with compassion. Our desire should always be to help them get back on their feet. That's why Galatians 6:1 says, "Brothers, *if someone is caught in a sin, you who are spiritual should restore him gently. But watch yourself, or you also may be tempted.*" Read that verse again carefully. I could hardly write a more desperately needed prescription for today's church!

If we really understood what the Bible says about the wickedness of our flesh, we would never adopt attitudes like the Pharisees', who in their self-righteousness were so willing to stone the adulteress. We would not be like the "locker room preacher," always ready to point a pious finger and condemn. The church would not be known as "the only army which shoots its own wounded." It's no wonder that for many people who have fallen and need a place to admit their need and to seek help, the *last* place they would consider is their local church. The offices of secular psychologists are bulging with Christians who wouldn't dare admit to other Christians what is really going on in their lives. In my opinion it is the phoniness and self-righteousness that comes from misteaching on spiritual growth and the flesh which has brought about this situation.

As I acknowledged before, this whole discussion of indwelling sin is not a joy to hear. As a matter of fact, it is not much fun to write about either! But it is a necessary building block of growing in grace. We absolutely must come face-to-face with *our own inability* before we will ever turn to Christ for *His ability!* That's why there is no greater sign that a person is genuinely growing in grace than when with humble tears he discovers the reality that he is a "wretched man." The only people who know this with a real heart understanding are those who are coming to know the Lord Jesus in an intimate way.

As we gain a clear-sighted, true understanding of ourselves up against the perfect righteousness of Christ, we see that we all fall miles short of the glory of God (Romans 3:23). It is a natural response: The more clearly we see the righteousness of God, the more we see our own sinfulness in reflection. But when we have an understanding of our identity in Christ and of His acceptance of us, this discovery does not bury us. It causes us to give humble thanks for the mercy and grace of our Lord and Savior and deepens our understanding of our need to live dependently on Him. From that thankfulness we grow to love Him more and to know Him more intimately. We continue to "grow in the grace and knowledge of our Lord and Savior Jesus Christ" as we abide in Him who is full of grace and truth.

EIGHT

∞

Sustained by Hope

I came home from work one day to find Amy crying. When I asked her what was wrong, she gave me the universal answer: "Nothing." The fact was, I really didn't need to ask Amy what was wrong; I had a pretty good clue already.

It was during a period in our lives when my father, whom Amy dearly loved, had died of cancer; my brother-in-law, Joe, had died of cancer; my sister-in-law, Betsy, had died of cancer; and our next-door neighbor was dying of cancer, being much evidenced by the screams of pain that we often heard in the middle of the night. On top of all this, Amy's brother-in-law, Mike, was also dying of cancer.

Obviously the deaths of our loved ones were sad situations, but the immediate cause of her sadness was Mike, who was still alive.

We talked for a long time, and finally I said to Amy, "Honey, let me see if I can paint a picture of what you are thinking right now. Are you imagining Mike in his coffin and your sister standing there crying, and your mother standing there crying, and all of our family standing there crying?" Amy looked up and said, "Yes, that's what I have been thinking."

I said, "Honey, it's no wonder you're feeling so sad. That is a very sad thought. But it's not a true thought. It is pure fantasy, and the only cure for fantasy is a return to truth."

I picked up the phone and said, "Why don't we call Mike right now and talk to him?" I dialed the number, and Mike's friendly voice came over the wires. "Hi, Mike," I said. "Amy and I were just wondering how you're doing."

"I'm doing pretty well," he answered. "In fact, this has been one of the better days I've had in a while." Amy and I took turns talking to Mike, and before long we were all enjoying a fun time of conversation that erased the terrible images that seemed so real to Amy a short time before.

This story illustrates again some things we have already discussed, such as the power of the mind to create vivid pictures that engender overpowering emotions, and therefore our need to fill our minds with truth. It reinforces the Lord's admonition that we live one day at a time (Matthew 6:34). We simply are not built to carry the burdens of the future. But more than that the aftermath of this story shows the importance of another biblical building block for growing in grace.

Within the next year Mike did die. But the reality, when it came, bore no resemblance to the imaginary scenario that drove Amy to despair. Upon getting the news of his death, Amy and I flew to Pennsylvania with great concern for Anna and their children. But when we got there we found a family being sustained by the grace of God. "Don't worry about us, little sister," Anna said. "We're doing all right." Even with eyes brimming with tears, she was able to say, "Mike is with Jesus, and his suffering is over. Death can separate us for a while, but we'll be together again one day with the Lord." Over the following days we all experienced what the Lord told the apostle Paul: "My grace is sufficient for you" (2 Corinthians 12:9). Yes, we grieved. Yes, we missed Mike, and we shed tears over our own loss. But the Christian who has his mind on the truth of Jesus Christ has something that the world does not have and cannot give: hope.

I want to say this carefully, because it can be easily misunderstood: Make no mistake about it—death is the enemy. To be a Christian does not mean that we are untouched by suffering. There is nothing "unchristian" about grieving over the death of a loved one! But normal grief is not the same thing as despair or depression. What sets the believer apart from the world at such times is his possession of truth from God that elevates him above life's circumstances.

It is hope that gives us God's perspective on life. Paul wrote, "Brothers, we do not want you to be ignorant about those who fall asleep [die], or to grieve like the rest of men, *who have no hope*" (1 Thessalonians 4:13). Death is a reality in this world. The true mortality rate is 100 percent. For those who deny the living God, death can only be a fact bringing stark terror and despair. But to the child of God death is simply an entrance into ultimate life in the presence of our heavenly Father: "absent from the body and ... at home with the Lord" (2 Corinthians 5:8 NASB).

In the meantime we live in a world where according to Jesus we will surely have trouble (John 16:33). Some trials and tribulations simply come from living in this fallen world and are those which are common to man. Some trouble is the unique variety that afflicts a child of God living in an unbelieving world. Some of our trials are internal—the "Romans 7" type— as we yearn to grow in grace, but find sin still firmly rooted within us. Whatever the brand of struggles we face, we need a secure hope in order to "hang in there" over a lifetime of growing in grace.

But what is hope? What does it mean, and how does it relate to growing in grace?

Part of our confusion arises because of the watered-down version of "hope" that we use in everyday speech. We say, "I hope I get a promotion at work." A child may say, "I hope I get a puppy for Christmas." "I hope it doesn't rain today," says the golfer. In each of these examples that "hope" describes the desire or wish of the individual, but it is used for things that are *uncertain*. Expanded, the thought of the person would be, "I don't know for sure if I'll get promoted. Maybe I will and maybe I won't, but I sure hope I will."

In contrast, the biblical meaning of hope is a solid, clear-thinking, totally thrilling truth. In the Bible, *hope is man's eager expectation of something that God has promised will certainly happen in the future.* There is never any "maybe" or "hope-so" about it! True hope is where God said "This will be" and we live in excited anticipation until it comes to pass.

To go back to one of our everyday examples, it is as if a father said to his son, "I promise you, you're going to get a puppy for Christmas. I'm going to pick him up on Christmas Eve after you're asleep, and he'll be there under the tree when you wake up in the morning." There would no longer be any doubt in the child's mind. It's no longer "I hope I get a puppy" in that lukewarm, uncertain sense. Now the child can hardly contain himself. "Only four more days until I get my puppy. Only three more days and eight hours until I get my puppy. Only two more days . . ." It's not a question of *whether* he'll get his puppy; it's just a matter of time until the promise of his father becomes a reality.

In the Scriptures God has given us a huge number of truths about our riches in Christ, such as the fact that we have been given the "gift of righteousness" (Romans 5:17), and that we can come boldly to the throne of grace (Hebrews 4:16). Though we do not see these things with our natural eyes, God says that they are true *in the present;* therefore, we are to respond by *faith* right now, and act accordingly. However, there are many other things that God teaches us that have *not yet occurred* in time— things such as the rapture of the saints, Christ's second coming, and the setting up of His millennial kingdom. In regard to these we live by *hope.* They are not yet true in our earthly experience, *but they will certainly happen,* and we eagerly await their fulfillment.

Hope is of absolutely crucial importance when a person is engaged in a long-term difficult task. Take a common example, such as a musical instrument, a craft, or a sport. When does someone get tired of trying and give up something that he is trying to learn? When, as we would say, "He has lost hope." We mean by this that he has lost any expectation that he will continue to improve and succeed in what he is trying to do. He has decided, "I'll never make it." That's when he quits.

I once met a young man in his twenties named Joe. He had responded as sincerely as he was able to a gospel invitation when he was ten years old. His story is a perfect illustration of what happens to a sincere person who knows only that Christ died for him, but doesn't have a clue of what it means that Christ lives in him. In a letter filled with pain he wrote:

> As I got older, I began to wrestle with sexual lust. I confessed this sin over and over to God, but I never really let go

of it. . . . I grew tired of feeling guilty, fearful, and weird all the time, so I compromised with this sin. . . . I didn't enjoy feeling like a hypocrite, yet I wanted to fulfill my lusts. . . . The hypocrisy really began to catch up with me. I was doing one thing and believing another. I was double-minded.

Joe went on to describe his downward spiral of failure, then concluded with these thoughts:

I am pretty certain that I am not saved. Each day I grow more and more convinced that I've hardened my heart to the Lord's call far too long. That I've committed the 'sin unto death.' That I've rejected the Holy Spirit's drawing me. . . . I hope and pray that I have not sealed my fate by my obstinate, presumptuous choices. If I haven't, it will take a miracle for God to dispel this error that is in my understanding. I'm losing hope fast. My life is absolutely upside-down.

These are cries of unbelievable confusion and pain. Some people will say that Joe obviously is not saved (Joe himself isn't even sure), but don't jump too quickly to that conclusion. According to Joe's testimony, he sincerely responded to the gospel message as it was presented to him. The tragedy is that, if he did respond to Christ by faith (as I believe he did), Joe was given that day "everything he needs for life and godliness" (2 Peter 1:3), just as every believer has. His problem is not lack of power; he is being tripped up by ignorance and error. Remember that "truth sets you free"; therefore it is error that puts you in bondage. In particular, you see in Joe the results of not understanding the truth of "Christ in you, the hope of glory" (Colossians 1:27). Among the many things that stand out in Joe's letter, surely one of the most obvious is his desperation born of hopelessness. This is why, when I am counseling someone "in the pits" like Joe, my first objective is to restore his hope. The love and grace of God become the most relevant and important truths in all creation to a person who is at the point of despair.

There are few things that can produce hopelessness like being on a performance basis for acceptance. In other words, someone says, "I love you *if . . .*" "If you perform . . . are good enough . . . are successful enough . . . do enough for me, then I will accept you." Trying to earn someone's love and acceptance—whether it is a parent, spouse, child, or friend—eventually leads you to despair, because you can never rest. You can never do enough. And this emotional effect is magnified to huge proportions when the goal of a person's labor is to earn the acceptance of God.

I met Jackie at a training seminar. She was in her early fifties, and was a radiant Christian, but she told me that her joy was only recently acquired. She said:

> Growing up, I was always aware that there was a God. However, my concept was that He was a God that condemned, judged, pointed a finger, and just maybe loved me if I did everything right. And I tried to do what would please Him. But I kept failing and watching others do the same. I reached a point where I thought, "What is life all about?"

Hopelessness and bewilderment are the predictable results of having a conception of God like Jackie's. At another seminar I met Jeff, who put his experience this way:

> I first came to Christ through the message of God's grace. They told me, as the song says, that "Jesus paid it all." However, shortly afterward I found out what they really meant.

They really meant that Jesus made the "down payment" on my salvation, but it was now up to me to "pay the balance"!

Where is the hope in a message like this? It seems as if they're saying that Jesus only made it possible for me to earn and keep my own salvation. "Oh, we believe in grace. God loves you unconditionally if you keep all the rules." That's a contradiction in terms. Grace is absolutely free. If you pay for it or earn it, it is no longer grace at all.

For that matter, you could not even call it salvation, because the results would be in doubt. What if you could not swim and were drowning in the middle of a lake because your boat had capsized. I come along in my own boat, extend a hand, and say, "Grab my hand. I'll save you." You do respond, and I pull you into the boat. "Thank God," you think, "I'm safe." But then halfway to shore you offend me. You either say something I don't like or perhaps you aren't as grateful as I like. So I pick you up and throw you back into the water to drown.

The question is, have I saved you? No. You were never saved. All you had was a *temporary reprieve*. In order to say that I saved you, I would not only pull you out of the water but *take you to shore and plant you on dry ground!* Only then would you be saved from drowning.

When you begin to see how depraved human nature is apart from Christ, you also begin to see that God had to accomplish a *total* salvation for us. If He had left anything in our hands to perform, *none of us would make it*. We could never rejoice in a salvation that is in doubt. But when we see the marvelous hope that we have in Christ—that *His faithfulness, not ours, is our assurance*—we can overflow with thanksgiving. That's why Peter wrote:

Praise be to the God and Father of our Lord Jesus Christ! In His great mercy He has given us new birth into a *living hope* through the resurrection of Jesus Christ from the dead, and into an inheritance *that can never perish, spoil or fade*—kept in heaven for you, who through faith *are shielded by God's power* until the coming of the salvation that is ready to be revealed in the last time (1 Peter 1:3-5).

Several years ago we went as a family to Yosemite National Park for a vacation. My son, Bobby, who was only about six years old at the time, asked me to take him rock-climbing. Would it have made any sense at all for me to say, "Here, Bobby, *you grab hold of my hand*, and we'll go rock-climbing"? Of course not. A six-year-old does not have the strength, balance, or experience to fend for himself. I would have been a criminally negligent father to do such a thing. What I did was to *take Bobby's hand into mine*, and then we went rock-climbing. I'm not especially heroic, but I can tell you that I would have gone to my death over a cliff, if necessary, to preserve my son's life. I would never have trusted him to hold on to me. I intended to hold on to him!

In the same way, our salvation does not rest on our ability to hold on to God. *It rests on His faithfulness to hold on to us!* That is the assurance of which Paul spoke when he said:

Being confident of this, that *He who began a good work in you will carry it on to completion* until the day of Christ Jesus (Philippians 1:6).

It has always impressed me that even to the Corinthians—the church that was doing hardly anything right—Paul expressed this same confidence. He called them "saints," ones who had been "sanctified in Christ Jesus and called to be holy" (1 Corinthians 1:2), then went on to say that they were—

> awaiting eagerly the revelation of our Lord Jesus Christ, *who shall also confirm you to the end, blameless in the day of our Lord Jesus Christ.* God is faithful, through whom you were called into fellowship with His Son, Jesus Christ our Lord (1 Corinthians 1:7-9 NASB).

When you read 1 Corinthians and see the abuses and errors of that church, Paul's confidence in their destiny seems incredible. But it all depends on where you are looking. *We* tend to look at behavior, but *Paul* was looking at the real source of our confidence: "*God is faithful.*" It is because of *His* faithfulness that you and I have assurance.

The first area of our lives where God wants to build into us a secure hope is in our assurance of salvation. We are not always faithful, but He always is, and He is going to bring us safely to His kingdom. But we still experience the ups and downs of life in this world, and the frustrations of living with indwelling sin. How does hope relate to the ongoing process of growing in grace?

Kay was a beautiful girl in her mid-twenties who came to me for counseling about her alcohol problem. She told me about the painful experiences she'd had in trying to get free of alcoholism. Tears welled up in her eyes as she expressed her frustration.

I immediately asked Kay about her relationship with the Lord Jesus Christ, and she assured me that she had come to Christ as a young girl. For many years she would have been described as a very committed Christian, but that was before alcohol had taken a firm hold on her. She had been to many Christian and secular counselors for help.

I spent many hours talking to her about her identity in Christ. Kay was similar to thousands of other people I have talked to in her weak understanding of salvation. When I asked her what her understanding of the gospel was, she gave me the typical answer: "Jesus died for my sins."

"Is that all salvation means to you?" I asked, and she answered, "Yes." She was floored when I went on to explain to her that forgiveness of sins was only half of salvation. Christ's death for us—as marvelous as that was and is—is not the totality of salvation. "The wages of sin is death, Kay," I said, "and that's why Christ came to give us life. That's why He said, 'I am the resurrection and the *life*' (John 11:25). That's why He said, 'I am the way—and the truth and the *life*' (John 14:6). Our problem was that we were dead, and the only solution for death is *life*. The Bible says that Christ in you is your only hope of glory."

Many times in Christianity, between the Christ who *was* and the Christ who *will be*, there is a total absence of the Christ who *is*. Realizing the fullness of the truth that Christ is alive and living in us is what brings the reality that we are children of God into focus.

After many days in which we thoroughly covered this truth, I asked Kay a question: "Kay, are you a child of God or an alcoholic?" Her answer was, "I guess I'm both." I replied, "That's impossible. God didn't give you two identities, only one. You are either an alcoholic practicing Christianity, or you are a child of God with a drinking problem. But you can't be both at the same time."

I then explained further, "Kay, if you are truly an alcoholic, if that is truly your identity, what is the most natural thing to do?" "Take a drink," she answered. "What is the most *un*natural thing to do?" I asked. "Stay sober," she said.

"On the other hand," I went on, "if you are a child of God, what is the most natural thing for you to do?" "Stay sober," she answered. "And what would be the most *un*natural thing to do?" I countered. "Get drunk," she answered.

"Kay, do you see what I'm getting at? If you truly are an alcoholic, why would you come to me to get help? If an alcoholic is *who you really are*, enjoy your booze. Enjoy being hung over, and don't look at it as abnormal. It wouldn't be abnormal to act like a monkey if in fact you were a monkey, would it? On the other hand, if you are a child of God it is obvious that this behavior is inconsistent with who you are. And if you are a child of God then Christ is alive, living in you. He wants to renew your mind, teach you His truth, control your emotions, and direct your will to conform to Him and to His will—not to fulfill the desires of the flesh. *Your problem, Kay is not one of behavior; your problem is one of identity.*"

Kay's eyes got as big as silver dollars, and she exclaimed, "I've got it! What I have been doing is totally stupid, isn't it?"

When I hear a counselee refer to sin as "stupid," I'm convinced they've got it. That's a sign that a person is really beginning to see himself and his sin from God's perspective. I said to Kay, "You're right, Kay. If you think you are truly a child of God, the way you have been thinking and acting in regard to alcohol is absolutely stupid."

That conversation took place five years ago. Just a month ago Kay came by to say hello. She said to me with joy in her heart and a smile on her face, "Bob, I cannot believe the way I used to think. I have never gone back to those old habit patterns since I have come to know who I am in Christ. And more importantly, I haven't been struggling with whether or not I should drink."

When Kay understood the difference between her behavior and her identity, hope became a reality for her.

That is how hope sustains you. Once you understand your identity in Christ—once you believe that God has a certain destiny for you—you can face the daily trials and struggles of the Christian life with confidence.

In Hebrews 6:19 hope is called an "anchor for the soul." That is a tremendous image, the picture of an anchor giving security and stability to a ship in a midst of a storm. That is what hope does for us, and more. For example, look at the logical flow of Romans 5:1-5. After saying in the first two verses that we have been justified by faith in Christ, and that we therefore have peace with God and presently stand in His grace, Paul goes on to say:

> And we rejoice in the hope of the glory of God. Not only so, but we also rejoice in our sufferings, because we know that suffering produces perseverance; perseverance, character; and character, hope. And hope does not disappoint us, because God has poured out His love into our hearts by the Holy Spirit, whom He has given us (Romans 5:2-5).

Where do we get this quality of rejoicing in sufferings? Through our hope in Christ. In other words, we can remain steadfast, trusting God through present difficulties and pains, because we know the outcome. In a way God has shown us His "time television set." It is found in Romans 8:29,30:

For those God foreknew He also predestined to be conformed to the likeness of His Son, that He might be the
firstborn among many brothers. And those He predestined,
He also called; those He called, He also justified; those He
justified, He also glorified.

If God knew you before the foundation of the world (and
He did; no one comes to Christ and catches Him by surprise;
if you are a believer in Christ, you were foreknown), then what
is your destiny according to this passage? *To be conformed to the
image of His Son!* Not "maybe," not "hope-so," but absolutely certain! The destiny of every child of God is to be just like Christ,
which is what it means to be "glorified." God is telling us that it
is certain, that it is as good as done. That's why we can "rejoice
in the hope of the glory of God" (Romans 5:2).

Some people respond to this biblical teaching with objec-
tions. "You can't tell this to people," they say. "If you tell Christians that they can't be lost again, they won't live for God.
They'll take your grace as a license to go sin up a storm!" Is that
true? Absolutely not! *Not if Jesus Christ lives in them!* This is why
it is vital to understand that *salvation is not just forgiveness of sins,*
as wonderful and important as forgiveness may be. Salvation is
also *God giving you Christ's resurrected life through the act of regener-
ation.* It is vitally important to remember that the gospel is not
just the truth that Christ gave His life for you. Jesus Christ *laid
down* His life *for* you so that He could *give* His life *to* you so that
He could *live* His life *through* you!

A Christian is not just a forgiven sinner. God promised that
in the New Covenant "I will put my laws in their minds and
write them on their hearts" (Hebrews 8:10). Peter wrote that
we Christians have become "partakers of the divine nature"
(2 Peter 1:4 NASB). In other words, you and I share in God's life!

Paul wrote the staggering truth that "he who unites himself with the Lord is one with him in spirit" (1 Corinthians 6:17). No wonder the Bible says, "If anyone is in Christ, he is a new creation; the old has gone, the new has come!" (2 Corinthians 5:17).

An illustration that I shared in *Classic Christianity* is that of a butterfly. You begin with a lowly caterpillar, crawling along on the lowest plane of life. A caterpillar is simply not going to fly, no matter how much you threaten it, promise it rewards, or give it flying lessons. However, at a certain time a caterpillar weaves itself into a cocoon and later emerges as a butterfly. It is a totally new creature. Now it can fly.

In my life I have seen countless beautiful butterflies, but I have never heard this: Someone yells excitedly, "Hey, everybody, come look at this good-looking *converted worm!*" I've never heard that, have you? No, no one refers to a butterfly as a "converted worm," though, if you think about it, it *was* a worm and it was indeed "converted." Then why don't we call it a "converted worm"? Because we don't think of what it *was*; we call it what it is *now*—a butterfly.

I often hear Christians refer to themselves as "sinners saved by grace." To me that makes as much sense as referring to butterflies as "converted worms." Yes, I was a sinner by nature, and I was saved by grace through Jesus Christ, but the Bible now calls me a child of God! The Bible even calls me a saint, which means a "holy one." Did I get that way through my actions? Not a chance! It was through grace alone. I am a holy one in the eyes of God because of what Christ has done, not through anything I do. And since God has taken the initiative to make me totally acceptable in His sight, He has been able to impart to me His very life, changing my innermost desires and nature into conformity with His.

Therefore, even though the sin which indwells my flesh still pulls at me, and though my mind is still subject to error, deception, and discouragement, I can say with Paul, "In my inner being I delight in God's law" (Romans 7:22). In my deepest desires I can honestly say that I want to be everything that God wants me to be. I want to love Him, serve Him, and be used by Him to the fullest extent. These qualities extend from the new life that God implants in us at the moment of spiritual birth.

The message of our secure hope in Christ is not an "encouragement to sin" for the true child of God. It is fuel for his inner fire, and food for his deepest hunger—to be everything that God wants him to be. It is this hope that keeps us hanging in there over the long haul: "As we received mercy, we do not lose heart" (2 Corinthians 4:1 NASB).

You and I have been called to grow in grace. However, this means that we will experience trials, tribulations, and failures along the way. Only with a secure hope rooted in the faithfulness of God will we be able to weather the storms of life. The Christian life is *empowered by faith*—our attitude of total dependency upon the indwelling Christ to live out His life in and through us. However, it is also our total confidence that Christ will complete the work He began in us that enables us to persevere over a lifetime. Without hope, people give up. The Christian life must not only be empowered by faith; it must also be *sustained by hope*.

NINE

∽✕∽

Freedom from Guilt

For the first few months, Stewart felt that he had gotten off easy. After all, he had been responsible for the death of 18-year-old Susan in an auto accident. He had been drunk and plowed into her car on a New Year's morning, killing her instantly. He was caught and convicted of manslaughter and drunken driving, and on top of his criminal trial, Susan's family had filed a civil suit against him and won. But they requested an unusual and creative judgment. Though they had originally sued Stewart for 1.5 million dollars, they settled for 936 dollars.

However, those 936 dollars were to be paid in a specific way. Each Friday, the day Susan died, Stewart was to make out a check in her name for one dollar and mail it to the family. The 936 dollars were to be paid one dollar per week for 18 years, one for each year of Susan's life. Susan's family wanted Stewart to remember what he had done.

Stewart discovered, after his initial relief, that this payment system was not the lark it appeared to be. At first he began to grow weary of the ritual. Then it got worse. He found himself becoming depressed as he was reminded each and every Friday that he was responsible for a young woman's death. Writing her name on the check became more and more painful, and he stopped writing them.

The family instantly went back to court to force him to continue. Four times during the next eight years Stewart stopped paying and was forced to start again by court order. Finally, testifying that he was "haunted by Susan's death and tormented by the payments," Stewart went to court himself to appeal the "cruel" punishment that had been levied on him. In court he offered Susan's family two boxes of checks covering payments for the remainder of the 18 years, plus an extra year. The family refused.

"What we want," they said, "is to receive that check every week on time. We will pursue this until those years are completed, and we'll go back to court every month if we have to."

When I first heard of this real-life story from news reports, I immediately saw many gripping parallels to biblical truths. *It illustrates pointedly why a Christian absolutely must come to an understanding of God's forgiveness and acceptance in Christ before he can go on to grow in grace.*

Think about Stewart's situation. As long as he is required to remember his crime and continue to pay a weekly debt to Susan's family, what do you think are the chances that he could ever develop a positive *personal relationship* with them? None! Paying that weekly check forces Stewart to concentrate on his past, and produces continued guilt and regret. His cry is, "I just want to get on with my life," but his weekly ritual will not let him. As long as this is true, he'll want to stay a million miles away from that family. *You cannot enjoy a personal relationship when guilt stands between the parties.*

Over the years I have met many pastors and other Christian leaders who wonder why their people will not give themselves freely to God for His use. It is no mystery to me. In many cases, *it is because they are dealing with God on the same basis as Stewart is with Susan's family.* They believe that there is still an unpaid debt between them and God, and that He must therefore be angry with them. As a natural result, they avoid Him. Their understanding of the forgiveness of their sins is more like the atonement offered under the Old Covenant than the completed work of Christ. They believe that they are forgiven up-to-date, but they are still paying on the balance.

I like to state the principle this way: *Until you rest in the finality of the cross, you will never experience the reality of the resurrection,* which is Christ Himself living in and through you! Unless you rest in the fact that Jesus did it all, you'll be so busy trying to "pay off your debt"—atone for your sins—that you'll never grow in and enjoy the personal relationship that Christ has provided for you. Let's explore why this is so, and examine some of the truths in which we must abide in order to continue growing in grace. The necessary background for these truths is an understanding of the Old and New Covenants.

If you were to read straight through the New Testament book of Hebrews, one word would continue to jump out at you: "*better.*" Though the Old Covenant (also called the law of Moses) was clearly given by God, it was a *temporary* system to prepare Israel for the coming of the Messiah, who would bring in a new relationship between God and man that would be far superior. In Hebrews, Jesus Christ, the Son of God, is presented not only as being better in His Person, but He is better in His priesthood; He brought in a better covenant; He offered a better sacrifice; and all His works have been "founded on better promises" (Hebrews 8:6). The Person and work of Jesus Christ are better in every way! One of the most dramatic contrasts between the two covenants can be seen in the issue of forgiveness.

I need to make clear at the outset that at no time in history has any person received salvation in any way except by grace through faith. Old Testament people received eternal life in the same way that you and I do today: through trusting in the promises of a merciful God. This is what Hebrews 11 is all about. However, even though people of all eras have been saved in the same *manner*—through faith—God's way of dealing with people in various eras has differed.

Daily forgiveness came to the Israelite under the law through the sacrificial system. However, that system was limited in what it could accomplish. Hebrews 9 explains the difference:

> The gifts and sacrifices being offered *were not able to clear the conscience of the worshiper.* They are only a matter of food and drink and various ceremonial washings—*external regulations* applying until the time of the new order. . . . The blood of goats and bulls and the ashes of a heifer sprinkled on those who are ceremonially unclean sanctify them so that they are *outwardly clean* (Hebrews 9:9,10,13).

What *could* those sacrifices do? They could make the worshiper clean "outwardly" or "ceremonially." In other words, for the time being you could be restored to being an "Israelite in good standing" under the law. But what could these sacrifices *not* do? They could not "clear the *conscience* of the worshiper." In a nutshell, the Old Covenant sacrifices could make a person *externally* or *legally* clean, *but they could not reach the inside of a person, where his conscience lies.*

In chapter 10, the writer of Hebrews adds a few more insights:

> The law is only a shadow of the good things that are coming—not the realities themselves. For this reason it can never, by the same sacrifices repeated endlessly year after year, make perfect those who draw near to worship. If it could, would they not have stopped being offered? For the worshipers would have been cleansed once for all, and would no longer have felt guilty for their sins (Hebrews 10:1,2).

Under the old system, forgiveness was offered on an "up-to-date" basis. When a man was convicted by the law as a transgressor, he could receive forgiveness by offering the prescribed sacrifice in faith. On a national scale, the greatest festival was the Day of Atonement, when the high priest would present the offerings for the entire nation. However, this passage shows the limitation of that system. It could never make the worshiper "perfect." As proof of this fact, the writer goes on to point out that if the law could have made the person perfect, there would have been no need for further offerings. The person with the cleansed conscience would have gone on his way. But the fact that the rituals were "repeated endlessly" stood as a continual object lesson that this system was not God's final plan.

In fact, not only did those offerings not bring a complete relief, but—

> *those sacrifices are an annual reminder of sins*, because it is impossible for the blood of bulls and goats to take away sins (Hebrews 10:3,4).

This is the passage I thought of when I heard the story of Stewart. Like his dollar-a-week payments, the Old Testament worshipers had to make continual offerings for their guilt. But even though those sacrifices brought a certain amount of relief from the fear of punishment, they were at the same time an "annual reminder of sins." The Day of Atonement for the Israelite was not a day of rejoicing; it was a day of concentration on failures, of confessing and mourning over sins. It was a day of regret. Yes, the past was washed clean, but there was always tomorrow. *Nowhere in the law of Moses do you find a sacrifice that offers cleansing for tomorrow's sins.* Like Stewart, who couldn't pay his future dollar-a-week payments as a lump sum, the Israelite could not bring a sacrifice for his future failures. The best he could hope for was to be clean up-to-date.

In total contrast to this system, Jesus Christ has done it all!

> Day after day every [Old Covenant] priest stands and performs his religious duties; again and again he offers the same sacrifices, which can never take away sins. But when this priest [Christ] had offered *for all time one sacrifice for sins*, He sat down at the right hand of God (Hebrews 10:11,12).

Jesus Christ has dealt with sins once and for all. He is *seated*, in contrast to the Old Testament priests, who were *standing*. Why? Because His work is done. "By *one sacrifice* He has made *perfect forever* those who are being made holy" (Hebrews 10:14). Therefore God says that in the New Covenant "their sins and lawless acts I *will remember no more*" (Hebrews 10:17).

Christ has done for us what could never have been accomplished under the law. He has accomplished total and final forgiveness of sins for us—not just for the past (even the old system did that) but for our entire lives, including the past, present, *and future.*

The Bible goes on to explain the results in our lives of what Christ has done for us. After teaching how the Old Covenant sacrifices made the worshiper *outwardly* clean, the writer of Hebrews says:

> *How much more*, then, will the blood of Christ, who through the eternal Spirit offered himself unblemished to God, *cleanse our consciences* from acts that lead to death, so that we may serve the living God! (Hebrews 9:14).

The sacrifice of the Son of God is superior in that it was a once-and-for-all offering, in contrast to the law, which required endless, ongoing sacrifices. But there is more: Jesus' death for us is also superior because *through it God can reach where no ritual offering ever could—man's heart.* The law offered cleansing *externally*, but Jesus Christ can cleanse the *conscience* of man so that he can *"serve the living God."*

One place where you can see our common failure to understand the finished work of Christ is in our celebration of communion, the Lord's Supper. During a conference, a man named Justin raised this issue. "Isn't it true," he asked, "that if you take the Lord's Supper and you are *unworthy*, you will bring judgment on yourself? That's what I've been taught."

I asked him back, "Just what do you mean by being unworthy?"

"I'm not really sure," Justin responded, "but there was a lot said about 'unconfessed sin in your life' and the need to confess it and 'get right with God.'"

"Justin, I've heard that kind of teaching for years too," I said, "but that is based on a misuse of the Scriptures. It's based on a misquoting of 1 Corinthians 11:27. The verse doesn't say that *we* have to become worthy. You and I are not worthy, and we will *never* be worthy in ourselves. Worthy is the *Lamb*, not the sheep! The verse actually says, 'Therefore, whoever eats the bread or drinks the cup of the Lord *in an unworthy manner* will be guilty of sinning against the body and blood of the Lord.' Paul is not saying that the *people* must become worthy; he is telling them to examine the *way in which they are celebrating* the communion! That is because in Corinth they had some who were gorging themselves, getting drunk, promoting divisions, and in many ways making a mockery of the unity of the church, the body of Christ. That is what he is talking about."

Because of this common misuse of the verse, people tragically miss the wonderful picture of grace in the Lord's Supper. They examine themselves with morbid introspection, searching for and confessing sins, feeling painful regret. The dominant emotion is often *fear*. This is a tremendous perversion of what God intended, and it totally misses the true spirit of the Lord's Supper. In 1 Corinthians 10:16 Paul calls the observance a *"cup of thanksgiving"*! That's a far cry from a "cup of regret," or a "cup of morbid introspection." What has occurred too often is that the celebration of the Lord's Supper has become like the old Day of Atonement. But there should be a total contrast. On the Day of Atonement the Israelite was to remember and confess his *sins*; in the Lord's Supper we should be remembering *the forgiveness of our sins*! It is to be a true *celebration*—a time of joy, thanksgiving, and unity in recognizing that we are one in Christ.

You can also see here another of the consequences of failing to finalize the forgiveness issue: It produces a *total concentration on self*. After all, if I am not "right with God," then I had better figure out how to correct the problem! Under his dollar-a-week payment system, Stewart never thinks about Susan's family or developing a relationship with them. All he can think about is obtaining relief from his burden of guilt. In the same way, a Christian who fails to rest in Christ's total forgiveness can never go on to "grow in the grace and knowledge of our Lord and Savior Jesus Christ" (2 Peter 3:18). He too thinks only about finding relief from his own guilt. Great numbers of Christians desperately labor, trying to "get right with God." But the Bible says we *are* right with God, completely and solely because of Jesus Christ's *finished* work on the cross! If I have been given the "gift of righteousness" (Romans 5:17), and if by His sacrifice Christ has made me "perfect forever" in His sight (Hebrews 10:14), how can I get any "righter"? Jesus Christ has come to take away our sins once-and-for-all to free us from a concentration on ourselves, so that we can freely concentrate on knowing Him!

It is incredible that this good news is so strongly resisted by many Christians. "You're being light on sin!" they cry. "Don't you know that God is a righteous God? He hates sin!" Even when people do not actively resist the message, they often have trouble grasping it. Those who have religious teaching in their background have usually heard that God is "holy" and "hates sin," though they seldom know what those ideas mean. Therefore to many people God remains a vague, disapproving, and sometimes absolutely terrifying figure. Against these firmly implanted visions of an angry God the message of forgiveness of sins through God's mercy and love seems to them like a total contradiction.

But there is no contradiction in God. He is perfectly just, and He is also totally merciful. The biblical term that pulls these truths together is *propitiation*. This truth can be the key that unlocks your understanding of all that Christ has done for you.

The Bible says, "He Himself [Christ] is the propitiation for our sins, and not for ours only, but also for those of the whole world" (1 John 2:2 NASB). "Propitiation" is an unfamiliar word to most people; you don't hear it used much on the street.

However, it is vitally important in understanding the gospel and God's attitude toward you. The central meaning of the word is *satisfaction*. But who had to be satisfied? Who has the right to demand satisfaction because of the offense of man's sins? Only a holy, just God.

The Bible from beginning to end describes a God who loves mankind; who is forgiving, longsuffering, patient, and merciful in His dealings with our rebellious race. However, the same Scriptures also depict a God who is perfectly holy and absolutely just, who "does not leave the guilty unpunished" (Exodus 34:7). How can He do *both*? Granted that He loves man and wants to save him, how can He do so without compromising His holiness or relaxing His standards—in short, without denying Himself? The answer lies in that word "propitiation." To help me get a handle on this concept, God allowed me to go through a gut-wrenching, but eventually rewarding, personal experience.

Several years ago I had an employee named Wayne—a nice, likable young man whom I trusted implicitly. But through a series of unusual events I was smacked in the face by the realization that Wayne had been embezzling money. I went into the books, desperately hoping that it was all a mistake, but the more I looked, the more obvious the truth became. One of the hardest things I have ever had to do in my life was to call him into my office and confront him with what I had found out.

After much discussion and many tears the story unfolded. Because of serious problems and pressures with his own personal finances, he had given in to temptation. Guilt and fear had been eating him up. He actually felt great relief when he was caught, and there was no doubt in my mind that he was genuinely repentant.

I had no desire to prosecute Wayne; rather, I wanted to help him get back on his feet. However, those stolen thousands of dollars remained an issue. Wayne had committed himself to paying the money back and was making regular payments, but the amount was so large that it was like using a spoon to dig the Panama Canal. It looked insurmountable.

Wayne came to the conclusion that he should sell his home in order to get the money. As he was working out the sales contract with his real estate agent, she asked him, "Wayne, why do you want to sell your house?" He explained that he needed the money in order to repay a debt to our company, but without mentioning the reason for the debt. The real estate agent was touched by the thought of this man with a wife and small children having to sell his home and decided to make a generous offer. "Wayne," she said, "I would hate for anyone to lose his home for that reason. Let's forget about selling this house. I want to pay the money back for you."

Wayne came to see me with his exciting news. It did seem like an ideal solution on the surface, but something was bothering me. "Wayne," I said, "I think it's great that you could be free from this burden. But first, I need to know: Does she know *why* you owe the money?"

Wayne's face reddened, and he answered, "No. She only knows that I owe you that amount."

I shook my head. "Then I can't accept it. I believe that it would be wrong to allow this lady to pay your debt unless she were fully aware of what she was paying for. But, Wayne, if you will go tell her the whole story—that you actually stole this money—and she still wants to pay for it, then I could accept it."

Wayne swallowed hard and left. He went back to the woman taking along two of our board members as witnesses. It was a joy a few days later to receive a phone call from the woman, saying, "Bob, Wayne has told me everything. I know all about the money he stole. But I believe he has learned his lesson. I still want to pay his debt."

There was nothing more to say. "Then I'm satisfied," I replied. "You know what you're paying for. You're not being misled. I'll accept it, and write Wayne's debt off the books."

What an illustration of the gospel, I thought. Here was Wayne, the offender; I was the one offended; and here was a "redeemer" with the means and the mercy to intervene. Wayne owed a debt he could not pay; this woman paid a debt she did not owe. I was the offended party who, when certain just conditions were met, said, "I am satisfied." In other words, I was "propitiated." The debt issue was over. All that remained was the continuing process of helping Wayne grow and develop in his new life.

In the Bible we find the same roles: man, the offender; God, the offended one; and Jesus Christ, the Mediator. God is perfectly holy; He is perfectly just; He hates sin with a pure and utter hatred. Therefore, since God's justice demands satisfaction, there is only one way in which man could escape the judgment he deserves: He must have an innocent substitute to receive that punishment for him. That is the meaning of the cross! Jesus Christ, sinless in Himself, went voluntarily to the cross *to receive the full wrath of God* for your sins and mine, and thereby to set us free from judgment. He paid a debt He did not owe, because we owed a debt we could not pay! As Isaiah 53:5,6 said prophetically:

> He was pierced for our transgressions, He was crushed for our iniquities; the punishment that brought us peace was upon Him, and by His wounds we are healed. We all, like

sheep, have gone astray, each of us has turned to his own way; *and the Lord has laid on Him the iniquity of us all.*

Because Jesus has paid for all our sins through the cross, all a person can do is to receive this wondrous and free gift by faith. One of the most common accusations made against those who teach this pure gospel of the grace of God is "You're teaching a *cheap* forgiveness." "Easy believism," it is also called. That makes my hair stand on end. The forgiveness of my sins may have been free to me, *but it was not 'cheap' to the One who paid for it!* Some things are without payment, not because they are worthless, but because they are *priceless!* What payment could a person offer that could add to the value of the blood of the perfect Son of God?

To say that the holy justice of God is fully satisfied (propitiated) is *in no way* to say that God has compromised with sin or has relaxed His holy standards one inch. Let me explain: If you were to ask a group of Christians, "What does the cross demonstrate?" most would answer, "God's love." That's absolutely true! Romans 5:8 says:

> God demonstrates His own love for us in this: While we were still sinners, Christ died for us.

So the cross does indeed show the love of God: "For God so loved the world that He gave His one and only Son . . ." (John 3:16). But much less familiar to most Christians is what Paul wrote in Romans 3:25:

> God presented Him as a sacrifice of atonement [the one who would turn aside His wrath or, "as a propitiation" taking away sin], through faith in His blood. He did this *to demonstrate His justice.* . . .

Paul goes on to explain that God "did it to demonstrate his justice at the present time, so as to be *just* and *the one who justifies* those who have faith in Jesus" (Romans 3:26). Consider it this way: If God were not *love* would there have been a cross? No. He would have just let men go to hell. On the other hand, if God were not *just*, would there have been a cross? No. He would have just said, "Well, boys will be boys. I'll let it go by this time, but try to do better." Only in the pure gospel will you find God shown as He really is, as unlimited sacrificial love *in perfect harmony* with uncompromising justice.

Imagine a judge in his robe, gavel in hand, as he presides over cases all day in a local court. He calls for the next case, and there stands his own son, accused of a serious traffic offense. What is the judge's role? He must determine whether the defendant is guilty or innocent, and if guilty see that justice is carried out. In this case the evidence is conclusive. "Guilty as charged," says the judge. "The court commands the defendant to pay a fine of $500 or spend 40 days in jail." He taps his gavel. The case is closed and punishment has been declared. The judge has done his job. But then an unusual thing happens. The judge stands, removes his robe, and walks around to the front of the court. He pulls out his checkbook and writes a check to pay his son's fine. As a judge, he made sure that justice was honored; as a father, he paid his son's debt. Here you see a tremendous picture of how God could forgive sinners without compromising His perfect justice—the cross was God's answer to both.

To teach that Jesus did it all is not to be "light on sin." It is to say that *God poured out every ounce of His holy hatred and wrath toward men's sins upon His Son*, who was bearing our judgment for us. Now, because Christ did pay it all, God can say that He is fully satisfied, and can deal with us without judging us for our sins: "Since we have now been justified by His blood, how much more shall we be saved from God's wrath through Him!" (Romans 5:9). Now, because God's justice is satisfied, we can live in freedom from fear:

> There is no fear in love. But perfect love drives out fear, because fear has to do with punishment. The man who fears is not made perfect in love (1 John 4:18).

Because we have been freed from the fear of punishment, we are free to grow in love for Him: "We love because He first loved us" (1 John 4:19). And because we have received the cleansing of our consciences, "we may serve the living God" with joy (Hebrews 9:14).

These are just some of the riches bound up in that small phrase "in view of God's mercy" (Romans 12:1). We are not like Stewart, in desperation and hopelessness bound to the past as we try to keep an "up-to-date account" with God. The only "account" we will ever have in God's eyes has been fully and forever supplied with the righteousness of Jesus Christ. Like Wayne, we owed a debt we could not pay, but we were set free by Someone who was willing to pay a debt He did not owe!

Therefore, when we present ourselves to God as living sacrifices, we are not presenting ourselves to an *enemy*, whose motives and purposes are suspect at best. We are presenting ourselves to a loving, wise, and powerful heavenly Father, whose motives and purposes for us are founded in His perfect goodness. "If God is for us," wrote Paul, "who can be against us? He who did not spare His own Son, but gave Him up for us all— how will He not also, along with Him, graciously give us all things?" (Romans 8:31,32).

"Therefore," Paul wrote, "I urge you, brothers, in view of God's mercy, to offer your bodies as living sacrifices, holy and pleasing to God—this is your spiritual act of worship" (Romans 12:1). As we grow in grace and in the knowledge of what Jesus Christ has done for us, it becomes increasingly clear that the most natural and reasonable thing to do is to give ourselves without reserve to our Lord for His use. But we absolutely must rest by faith in the complete acceptance that Jesus has purchased for us if we are going to continue growing in grace. Unless we rest in the finality of the cross, we will never experience the reality of the resurrection—Christ living His life through us!

TEN

❧❀❧

Freedom and Maturity

Tim seemed to be a reasonably mature, stable teenager as he prepared to go off for his first year of college. He always looked clean and neat, he was polite, and he did well enough in his high school studies to be accepted by a good university.

It was a real shock to see the contrast between the boy who left in August and the boy who came home for Christmas vacation after the first semester. His once-neat, medium-length hair had become long, dirty, and shapeless. He had gained 25 pounds. He wore a dirty, smelly T-shirt and jeans, both checkered with holes. His tennis shoes were rotting away, and their pungent smell preceded him into a room. Tim's mother was also less than thrilled to discover that he had brought home with him a large laundry bag full of clothes, towels, and sheets for her to wash—none of which gave any evidence of having been laundered since he had left the previous summer! Tim's father, on the other hand, contemplated the fact that his son, who had always gotten A's and B's through public school, had managed at college to achieve one C and three D's, and had avoided an F only by dropping a course before the final exam.

What had happened to Tim? Are these the usual results of a young man going off to college? If so, you might conclude, let's not send our children there. But we had better take a closer look at the facts before we draw a hasty conclusion. In particular, we need to examine what Tim seemed to be *before* leaving for the university.

I mentioned that Tim had seemed to be a reasonably mature 18-year-old, but on closer examination that appearance turned out to be artificial. He always did look neat and clean, but that was because his mother did his laundry and insisted that he wear clean clothes, and his father supervised his haircut and style. The polite manners that he displayed turned out to be the result of a lot of nagging and dire threats from Mom and Dad. His acceptable grades in high school were generated because his parents strictly enforced curfew rules, demanded to see daily work, and promised money and privileges for A's and B's.

In short, what looked like qualities of maturity and character in Tim were in reality a mere facade that was propped up by Mom and Dad. He really had very little character of his own, and that was proven by what happened when Mom and Dad were taken out of the picture: Tim immediately collapsed into a fat blob of immaturity. Without Mom to do his laundry, it didn't get done. Without Dad to make him do his studies, Tim didn't do them. Without anyone telling him when to go to bed, Tim stayed up to all hours, went to late-night fast-food restaurants, and slept through his morning classes. When he came home for Christmas vacation, he exhibited the fruit of four months of undisciplined, unrestrained, immature living.

Did college make him that way? Absolutely not! All going away to college did was to reveal the lack of character in Tim *that was already there* by removing his artificial props called parents. In other words, freedom did not *make* Tim immature; it *revealed* the immaturity in him that already existed.

Happily, in Tim's case, he came to his senses. He looked in the mirror and said, "If I don't want someone to paint 'Goodyear' on my side, I'm going to have to lose some weight. If I don't want to flunk out of college, I'm going to have to study and get to my classes. And if I don't want to smell like a barnyard, I'm going to have to learn to do my own laundry."

He didn't grow up overnight, but he did begin growing. He started jogging, and quit eating at two in the morning. He started studying and did make at least some of his morning classes. He did learn how to do his laundry, and though not a fashion plate, he looked clean. He came home from his second semester slim again, with a B-minus average, and a lot wiser. He had finally begun the process of growing in maturity to become a "self-starter," no longer dependent upon someone standing over him with a club or offering him "a piece of candy" to live in a responsible, adult manner.

The reason I have gone to such length to explain Tim's experience is because it parallels in a remarkable way some of the issues and problems that people face in growing in grace.

For almost 2000 years the church has been plagued by the pressures to return to Galatianism. Remember that Galatianism is, after having come to salvation by faith, returning to the law in an effort to perfect yourself. The greatest practical problem you face in persuading people to abandon Galatianism is that *putting people under the law produces an appearance of maturity and character in them.* But, like Tim's example under the "law of Mom and Dad," that appearance is an artificially supported facade. As Paul pointedly says in Colossians 2:23:

> Such regulations indeed *have an appearance of wisdom*, with their self-imposed worship, their false humility and their harsh treatment of the body, *but they lack any value in restraining sensual indulgence.*

In other words, Paul is saying that adherence to laws can make a person look good on the *outside*, but it cannot change a heart or build internal character. Therefore laws cannot produce true growth in grace. In fact, they actually *work against* the process of growing in grace, because the Bible says, "*The power of sin is the law*" (1 Corinthians 15:56). As long as people are kept under the law, *they are kept under the power of sin.* The law not only is powerless to change a heart, but it actually *stirs up* sinful desires in us:

> I would not have known what sin was except through the law. For I would not have known what coveting really was if the law had not said, "Do not covet." But sin, seizing the opportunity afforded by the commandment, produced in me every kind of covetous desire. For apart from the law, sin is dead" (Romans 7:7,8).

Is this because the law is bad? Absolutely not! "The law is holy, and the commandment is holy, righteous and good" (Romans 7:12). The problem is *us*. The law demands perfect performance, and we cannot comply; therefore the law declares our guilt:

> Now we know that whatever the law says, it says to those who are under the law, so that every mouth may be silenced and the whole world held accountable to God. Therefore no

one will be declared righteous in His sight by observing the law; rather, *through the law we become conscious of sin* (Romans 3:19,20).

God gave the law to convict us of our guilt and our need for a Savior, so that we would turn to Jesus Christ by faith: "So the law was put in charge to lead us to Christ that we might be justified by faith" (Galatians 3:24). But once the law has brought us to Christ, it has accomplished its purpose: "Now that faith has come, we are no longer under the supervision of the law" (Galatians 3:25).

That's why Paul said in another context, "We know that the law is good *if one uses it properly*" (1 Timothy 1:8). Like a hammer that can be used by a carpenter to build a house or be used by a murderer to crush someone's skull, the law can be used properly or improperly. The law is a blessing from God in its proper use, as a mirror to show us the truth about ourselves so that we will see our desperate need for total dependency upon Jesus Christ. However, the law can also destroy when it is misused, and *it is misused when it is used to produce an outward conformity in the absence of faith, hope, and love.*

The ultimate practical proof that the law is useless to produce Christ's life—the fruit of the Spirit—can be seen when it is abruptly removed *from the teaching of Christ living in and through you.* You'll sometimes see Christians reacting to their newfound "freedom" much like Tim did when he finally escaped from Mom and Dad: They go wild. Then the accusation comes, "See what happens when you don't keep people under the law? They go out and live like the devil. That's what the teaching on freedom produces!"

No! *That's what keeping people under the law produces—a total lack of Christian maturity.* Taking them out from under the law merely *reveals* the lack of character in them that already existed. The teaching of God's grace does not *make* people spiritually immature any more than going away to college made Tim immature.

It reminds me of the contrast between a city dog and a country dog. Have you ever had a dog that you kept in the house, or perhaps kept penned in the backyard? What happens when there is a momentary crack in the doorway or fence? He's out of there like lightning! Give him a glimpse of freedom, and he's gone. I remember a dog we once had who would be charging up the street as I ran behind him calling his name. Did he stop? No way. He would actually turn and seem to grin at me as he ran away from me. The more I chased him, the faster he ran.

On the other hand, have you ever seen a country dog? Picture "Old Duke." There are no fences, but only miles of pasture and forest to run in. He can go wherever and do whatever he wants. Where is he? Right smack on the front porch of the house, sleeping contentedly! He is happy to hang around the house, waiting for his master to come play, or take him hiking or hunting.

People are the same way. They cannot stand to be in bondage. They may remain in captivity if there are enough strong threats, persuasive deceptions, or peer pressure, but if you give them a crack of freedom in this situation they are out of there like a city dog. That is exactly what Tim did, and that is exactly what Christians who have been kept penned up by legalism often do when they first hear about freedom in Christ. Without a personal understanding of the grace and truth found in Jesus Christ to guide them, they see freedom only as an opportunity to indulge the flesh.

Christians are often quick to condemn people who are "rebelling against God" without first looking more closely and asking, "What are they really rebelling against?" Usually people are actually rebelling against the legalistic religion that has kept them in bondage, not against God Himself. When the city dog is running up the street, is he really running away from his master? No, he's running away from the *fence*. He normally loves his master. He just hates being penned up. More times than I can count I have found myself talking with "rebellious Christians." When I say, "Tell me about this God you are rebelling against," they tell stories of ugly religion, pressure to conform, and man-made standards. My response usually shocks them: "Good! You *should* be rebelling against those things! They're not the true God, and that's not what Jesus Christ meant when He said He came to give us abundant life." I find that these "rebels" are some of the most excited, dynamic believers I know once the errors of legalism have been corrected.

But it is important that we emphasize what God has *added* above and beyond the removal of the law. To release someone from the captivity of law without adding something in its place is like letting the city dog out of his pen. He'll just take off running as fast as he can to get away. God's method of releasing us from the law is by replacing it with His indwelling life. Why does the country dog stay near the front door when he has miles of freedom? Because he knows and loves his master. His freedom is not freedom *from* bondage, but freedom to be *with* the one he loves. In the same way, as I grow to know and love Jesus Christ more intimately I find myself experiencing incredible freedom and hardly think about the law at all. The issue is not what I *can* or *cannot* do. I am free to know my heavenly Father in an unhindered personal relationship. That's what I concentrate on. Then through that relationship God teaches my mind to think His thoughts. Where I am wrong, he *reasons* with me. He doesn't lock me back behind the fence!

In Romans 6:15 Paul anticipates and raises the question that every teacher of grace hears time and time again: "What then? Shall we sin because we are not under law but under grace?" That question expresses the characteristic attitude of a person who knows only law, and who has not come to experience Christ living through him. To answer, Paul reasons:

> When you were slaves to sin [before you came to Christ by faith], you were free from the control of righteousness. *What benefit did you reap* at that time from the things you are now ashamed of? Those things result in death! (Romans 6:20,21).

People say some of the most thoughtless and foolish things in response to the message of God's love and grace. "If you teach people that they are totally forgiven," many say, "then they will go out and sin like the devil." I reply, "When did the law ever *stop* people from sinning?" Others ask, "If what you are saying is true, that God accepts us in Christ regardless of our actions, then why shouldn't I just sin up a storm?" In response to such foolishness I feel like replying, "If that really is your attitude, go ahead. Then in a little while you can come back and *tell me* why not!" What questions like these unmistakably reveal is the slender, meager experience which the questioner has had of the indwelling abundant life of Jesus Christ. Asking if we "should sin because we are under grace" is like someone facing an abundant cafeteria line and asking permission to go eat out of garbage cans!

In Galatians 4:1-7 Paul uses an illustration from the everyday Greek and Roman world to illustrate the role of the law in relation to growth in maturity. He begins with an observation built on common family life of his time:

> What I am saying is that as long as the heir is a child, he is no different from a slave, although he owns the whole estate. He is subject to guardians and trustees until the time set by his father (Galatians 4:1,2).

Imagine yourself as the small, four-year-old son of a wealthy Roman citizen during the New Testament period. Your father owns many acres of property, with houses, barns, cattle, horses, and crops. He also has many investments, both local and abroad. Living on the property as well are several dozen slaves. However, you are his only child. In the eyes of your family as well as your father's business associates, friends, and slaves, who are you? There is no question about it: *You are the heir.* All that your father owns will someday be yours, and everybody knows it. But there is a catch: Four-year-olds do not manage the family business. They are not ready for adult life.

Therefore your father would follow the common practice of the time, and appoint one of his household slaves as your "guardian" or "trustee." That slave, as long as you are a child, has total authority over you. He can make you do things you don't want to do, and he can stop you from doing things you do want to do. He exerts control over what you eat and where you go, and he supervises your education. In fact, that slave so dominates your life that you feel in your experience as if *you* are the slave! That is why Paul said in verse 1 that "as long as the heir is a child, he is no different from a slave."

However, there is no question about who you actually are: *You are always the heir of all your father's wealth.* And up ahead is that date set by your father when you will no longer be a child, but will assume adult status. And on that great day your father will throw a huge celebration, inviting friends, relatives, and business associates. This is to celebrate your *adoption.* That sounds peculiar to our ears, because we think of adoption as joining a new family. However, in the Roman world adoption stood more for the assumption of adult status and the designation of a person as an heir. Like a Jewish bar mitzvah, or social "coming-out party," this is your entrance into the adult world. Your father places on you for the first time a toga, the robe worn by adult males, and he announces, "My son, who was once a child, is now a man." Whereas you were once under slaves and were treated like one yourself, now you are the master over them. You can move in society as an adult, and you can now transact business. You are, in effect, co-owner of your family property with your father.

Why does Paul call up this elaborate illustration? Because he is going to use it to show the big picture of God's working with men through the ages. He goes on to say, speaking of the nation of Israel:

> So also we, while we were children, were held in bondage under the elemental things of the world. But when the fulness of time came, God sent forth His Son, born of a woman, born under the Law, in order that He might redeem those who were under the Law, that we might receive the adoption as sons (Galatians 4:3-5 NASB).

In other words, God made it clear for hundreds of years that the nation of Israel would one day inherit the promises made through the prophets, *but the time of maturity had not yet come.* Therefore God also put His chosen nation under "guardians and trustees," which was the law of Moses. The Mosaic law stood in the same relationship to Israel as the appointed household slave did to the young heir of the family. Paul refers to the law as "the elemental things of the world," meaning roughly the ABC's or the elementary school of God's plan.

Then, following the death and resurrection of Jesus Christ, God hosted His adoption ceremony and His people's "coming-out party." We know it as the Day of Pentecost. That was when the people of God came into their time of maturity, and now our "toga" or mark of adulthood is the fact that we have received the Holy Spirit of God:

> Because you are sons, God sent the Spirit of his Son into our hearts, the Spirit who calls out "Abba, Father." So you are no longer a slave, but a son; and since you are a son, God has made you also an heir (Galatians 4:6,7).

To say that the Christian is not under the law is not to insult the law or say that it is bad. For people who lived in the Old Testament period, being a member of God's Covenant people was an unspeakable blessing. The entire world had sunk into spiritual darkness, ignorance, and paganism. But in that world, one nation—Israel—knew the true God. Because they had God's Word, they knew the truth about God, themselves, right and wrong, and the future. God intended them to be a light in a dark world. The Old Covenant did indeed "come with glory" (2 Corinthians 3:7).

However, "*What was glorious* [the law] *has no glory now in comparison with the surpassing glory*" [of the New Covenant]

(2 Corinthians 3:10). Again, to say that we are not under the law is not to downgrade the law; *it is to maintain that something better has come!*

More specifically, God used the law to manage His chosen people in the centuries before Christ. But ever since the coming of the Spirit at Pentecost, we live in a different age. *Rather than managing His people by law, God now wants His people to grow in grace through the leading of the Holy Spirit.* This is why Galatians 5:18 says, "If you are led by the Spirit, you are not under law." To be "led by the Spirit" means that we Christians have the privilege of walking in a loving, trust relationship with our heavenly Father! His goal is to grow us in grace as a result of our personal relationship with Him, not to "keep us in line" under the law.

Once the young heir has had his public adoption ceremony and entered the adult world, what sense would it make for him to allow himself to be bossed around by that same slave who had managed him during his childhood? Should the slave continue to stand over him, giving him orders, telling him what to eat, where to go, and what to do? If you were a family friend observing such a scene, you would think it tragic. It would be absolutely unfitting for the slave to be master over the adult son. Though the son's behavior would look good superficially, such a situation would guarantee his continued immaturity. He would never grow up.

The very same thing is true for the Christian. God gave the law to His people in their time of immaturity, but now that we have come into the position of adult sons in the kingdom, He does not want us to return to the domination of the law. To do so would be to guarantee that we would never grow in grace. It is a predictable fact: Keeping Christians under the domination of the law is to ensure their continued spiritual immaturity.

We have to make the same decision that parents have to make regarding their children: If we want them to grow up, we will have to allow them the freedom to make some mistakes. Parents who are so petrified that their children might make some wrong decisions or experience some personal tribulations that they smother them with parental control actually ensure that their children will never develop an ounce of character.

I often ask groups, "Where did you learn the most valuable lessons that you have learned in life?" Without exception people respond, "Through falling flat on my face." I then ask, "Then what makes you think your children will grow in character without going through personal trials and tribulations? The Bible says that 'tribulation brings about perseverance; and perseverance, proven character' (Romans 5:3,4 NASB). Obviously as parents we want to protect our children from the most dangerous things of the world, but we cannot and should not try to protect them from all personal tribulations. If we do, they will be totally unprepared to enter the real world as adults. They will have neither the experience nor the maturity to make it on their own."

Going through trials is how we grow! Yes, if you teach the freedom that is ours in Christ, there are a certain number of immature people who will try to take advantage of it—for a while. But by falling flat on their face, they will learn how stupid sin really is. However, if we are teaching people how to walk according to the indwelling life of Christ, *those will be the exception, not the rule.* People are looking for real life, and it is found in Jesus Christ. People living under law are like the "city dog," who at the first crack of freedom will be gone. People living under God's grace and who are experiencing Christ living in and through them are like the "country dog." They can still fall to various temptations, since they still live with indwelling sin, but since they are not under the law, sin begins to lose its "forbidden fruit" appeal. Their deepest desire is to walk in a close love relationship with the Lord. Because of His constant love, when they *do* fall they get back up and return to dependency upon Christ, and continue to grow in grace.

Remember that a child of God is not just a forgiven sinner! The Spirit of God has come to live in him, making him alive in Christ. And Christ is committed to renewing our minds according to His truth. Remember: *He* is still faithful (even when *we* aren't!). People often ask, as Jill did recently on our radio program, "But what about those times when we walk away from God?"

I answered, "You may *think* you're walking away from God, but God never leaves you! *He lives in you.* How can you walk away from someone who lives *in* you, and who promised, 'Never will I leave you; never will I forsake you'? (Hebrews 13:5). We may be deceived and feel beaten down, but His love and grace continue to draw us to Himself, and He continues to fulfill His promise: 'He who began a good work in you will carry it on to completion until the day of Christ Jesus'" (Philippians 1:6).

After giving his witness to Jesus as the Messiah, John the Baptist remarked, "He must increase; but I must decrease" (John 3:30 NASB). That is a good way to describe what growing in grace is like. Many times when you hear people talk about "growing in spiritual maturity," you get the impression that they are getting bigger and stronger. But the truth is exactly the opposite. To truly be growing in Christ means that we are becoming less and less, and He is gaining greater access to our lives. This often happens through trials and tribulations: They cause us to depend totally on Christ and His sufficiency rather than relying on our own. When we come face-to-face with our own inadequacy, we are forced to turn to Him for His total adequacy.

An incident in my own family illustrated for me the power of unconditional love and acceptance in an atmosphere of freedom, and how God can take even our failures and cause them to work together for good.

I came home from work one day to find my wife, Amy, and my son, Bob, sitting in the living room. Amy was crying her eyes out, and Bobby looked as simple as a horse. He looked bleary-eyed, pale, and sick—which he was. It was the last day of school, so he and some buddies had decided to really celebrate. They got hold of some beer, which Bobby had never tried before, and made it their goal to get rip-roaring drunk. Bobby had gone along with the guys and was now paying the price. He had thrown up everything but his toenails, and I think he was working on those. He was positively green.

I had only a few seconds to decide how to respond, and there were a lot of things that could have crossed my mind. I could have been outraged, since I was, after all a well-known minister. I was a Bible teacher and counselor, and I was on the radio every day talking about the Lord. I was a highly visible figure at a large church, which was known for being against alcohol consumption. If people found out what Bobby had done, it could reflect badly on me. Those are some of the things I could have thought. But the truth is, I thought about none of these. All I could see was my son whom I loved more than anything on earth. I immediately walked over and put my arms around him.

"Bobby," I said, "I love you. I hate what you did, but I love you."

We sat for a few minutes, and then Bobby said, "Daddy, let's pray." And we did.

Long afterward I learned what a significant experience this was in my son's life. A few years later, in a conversation where we recalled the occasion, Bobby said, "You know something, Dad? All my life you told me you loved me. But that day I *knew* you loved me."

Like any parent who loves his children, I wish Bobby didn't have to go through that experience. I wish he never had to experience pain and troubles at all—but that is not the world we live in. Jesus said, "In this world you will have trouble" (John 16:33). If he did have to fall on his face to learn some valuable lessons, I am so grateful that I have experienced God's unconditional love and acceptance in my own life so that I could pass it on to him. Bobby learned that drinking is not all that it is cracked up to be, and that it is not always smart to follow the crowd. Those lessons served to protect him and guide his decision-making in many future situations, and he has grown into a fine, mature young man. But, most importantly, he learned a lesson *through experience* about unconditional love and acceptance.

I wish it weren't so, but it is a fact that we learn the extent of God's love and grace in our lives through our personal failures. After we fall flat on our face, He lifts us up and we see that He still loves us and accepts us, even if He hates what we did. This causes us to be drawn to love Him more, and to trust Him more as we continue our walk through life. He appeals to us as grown children, *reasoning* with us to live according to the new life He has given us. As Paul said, "You, my brothers, were called to be free. But do not use your freedom to indulge the sinful nature; rather, serve one another in love" (Galatians 5:13).

In the face of such steadfast love, what can we do but continue presenting ourselves to the Lord to allow Him to work out His will in our lives? This is what Paul had in mind when he wrote:

> For *Christ's love compels us,* because we are convinced that one died for all, and therefore all died. And He died for all, *that those who live should no longer live for themselves but for Him who died for them and was raised again* (2 Corinthians 5:14,15).

Whether we are coming from a perspective of law or grace makes a dramatic difference when we are dealing with a situation like Bobby's getting drunk. The crucial question is, *What is your goal?* If I had had a law perspective, I would have ripped and punished him. My goal would have been to make sure he didn't drink again. *But is that God's goal?*

No! *God's goal is that His children grow in grace.* That is a much bigger goal than merely stopping a certain behavior. If my goal as a parent is the growth and well-being of my child, then the drinking issue is just an indicator. I want to know what's going on *inside.* "What are Bobby's hurts and needs?" I would wonder. "What is he thinking and feeling that has caused him to do this? Was it just foolish immaturity given an opportunity, or is it a sign of something deeper and more serious?" Those are the kinds of questions you ask *when you care about a person,* instead of just wanting to shape up his *behavior.*

God cares about *you.* There is nothing you can give Him, there is no service you can perform, there is no self-discipline you can apply that He wants more than He wants *you.* He wants to reveal Himself and His love to you, and He wants you to grow to love Him in return. This is how we grow in grace. However, for this to happen, it is essential that we abide in the truth of God's Word—particularly in those truths which deal with our total acceptance, forgiveness, righteousness, and life in Jesus Christ. Only by abiding in the truth that Christ has done it all can we have the boldness to approach God and get to know Him in a personal way. If we have a law mentality, it will never happen. We must *abide* in His grace in order to *grow* in His grace.

ELEVEN

Food for Growth

When I was a child, back in those years when I was still known as "Pee-Wee," I wanted desperately to grow. My mom would periodically measure my height against the wall in my room, and I would stretch as hard as I could to be a little taller. As I later became a parent, I saw my own children do the same thing. Every child, it seems, wants to grow up by the day after tomorrow, but it can't be done.

That is a frustrating thing to learn when your name around the neighborhood is "Pee-Wee." "But I want to get bigger," I would protest. "How can I make myself grow?" As a wise adult, what you would probably say is, "Son, you can't *make* yourself grow. Growing up takes *time*. But here's what you *can* do: You can eat good food, exercise, and enjoy being an eight-year-old. Don't be so worried about becoming a grown-up. Have fun right now being who you are. You'll grow up soon enough."

I find Christians who are worried and bothered to the point of making themselves absolute emotional wrecks, worried over the progress they think they should be making in their Christian growth. However, you cannot *make* yourself grow spiritually any more than you can make yourself grow physically. We forget that it is God who is in the business of conforming us to the likeness of Christ (Romans 8:29). We forget that it is *"he who began a good work in you [and] will carry it on to completion until the day of Christ Jesus"* (Philippians 1:6).

This is not to say that we have *no* decision to make or role to play. After all, the Bible says that we should "work out our salvation with fear and trembling" (Philippians 2:12). But we need to be clear on what that passage means. After saying in verse 12 that we should "work out" our salvation, Paul says, *"for it is God who works in you to will and to act according to His good purpose."* So once again we find that in the Christian life God *initiates* and *man responds.* In fact, my working definition of "responsibility" is "my *response* to God's *ability.*" A good way to paraphrase these verses is, "In a humble and dependent attitude, work out on the outside of your life what God is doing on the inside." We do not grow ourselves. God is inside of us "to will and to do according to His good purpose." Our role is to walk in an intimate, loving, faith relationship with our heavenly Father, and to cooperate with what He is doing in our lives.

You cannot make yourself grow physically, but you can "eat good food, exercise, and enjoy being an eight-year-old." In our spiritual lives, we cannot make ourselves grow in grace either, but we can do some things: We can eat good food, exercise, and enjoy walking through life as a child of God as He grows us in His time. But what do I mean by "eating good food and exercising?"

This is where I want to address some specific areas of the Christian life. I have deliberately left these subjects for the end of this book, even though most people would expect a book called *Growing in Grace* to have hit them hard from the beginning. These are the subjects of personal Bible study, prayer, and our relationships within the body of Christ.

The reason I have kept these subjects for the end is because of the terrible twisting that has been commonly done to them. We have taken these activities which should be natural and enjoyable overflows of our life in Christ and our personal relationship with Him, and turned them into *disciplines*. There is no greater way to ruin these wonderful privileges we have as children of God or to rob us of our joy in knowing Him than to view them as *disciplines*—things you *have* to do "in order to be a good Christian." In this chapter I want to discuss Bible study in detail. The other issues we will tackle in the next chapter.

When I was born again in Christ, I came to Him as a 36-year-old man who knew absolutely nothing of the things of God. I had no religious teaching in my background to speak of. All I knew the day I received Christ was that "God so loved the world that he gave his one and only Son, that whoever believes in him shall not perish but have eternal life" (John 3:16). I was simply overwhelmed with the idea that God actually loved *me*! And I opened up my Bible to learn more. In fact, over the next couple of years I buried myself in God's Word to the point that my wife, Amy, thought I had a black leather face!

Naturally, I did not understand it all. There were many parts of the Scriptures that were mysterious to me, and, as many young Christians do, I came up with some fanciful ideas and interpretations that seem silly to me today. But God did reveal Himself to me, and He did teach me a solid understanding of His Word over time. I look back at those early years of my Christian experience as some of the most joy-filled times of my life. I truly came to God as a little child and leaned totally on my heavenly Father to teach me.

Nobody told me I *had* to study the Bible, and I'm glad they didn't. Since "the power of sin is the law" (1 Corinthians 15:56), hammering people with what they "ought" to be doing is the most effective way to stir up rebellion and resistance in them. At the very least, it spoils your joy and freedom in Bible study when it becomes an *obligation* rather than a *privilege*. I never heard sermons putting me on a guilt trip for not studying enough. I didn't follow some scheduled program of study. It never occurred to me that I was doing something I was "supposed to do." I simply opened God's Word and read it, because that is what I *wanted* to do more than anything on earth. Let me pass on to you some tips that have helped many people discover the great experience of personally digging into the Word of God.

First, *read the Bible in order to get to know Christ, not just to learn Bible facts.* We have been called to a *relationship.* Jesus said, "Now this is eternal life: that they may *know you,* the only true God, *and Jesus Christ,* whom You have sent" (John 17:3). Paul wrote, "I consider everything a loss compared to the *surpassing greatness of knowing Christ Jesus my Lord*" (Philippians 3:8). Don't make the same mistake I did later, when I strayed from my personal relationship with Christ into dry knowledge and barren service. Don't get on that terrible treadmill of the "search for something more." Don't fall for the deception of believing that we start out with Christ, then "graduate" to the "deep things" of God. *Jesus Christ is everything.* There is nothing "deeper" than knowing Him intimately! That is what we will do throughout eternity—discover and enjoy the wonders of Him. We'll never get to the end of all that He is.

In all my years in school I never studied a textbook to get to know the author. For example, I studied my biology textbook to learn enough biology to pass the exam; I didn't know or care about the scientist who wrote it. However, the Bible is strikingly different here. The purpose of studying God's Word is, first and foremost, to get to know Him, the Author.

I have learned that if I go to the Bible merely to learn facts, I'll get those dry facts, but nothing else. However, if I go to the Bible desiring to meet personally with the Lord, He will open my heart to know Him, and teach me biblical facts at the same time. Every time I open my Bible, it is with this spoken or unspoken prayerful attitude: "Lord, I cannot understand this Bible unless you teach it to me. I certainly cannot know You unless You reveal Yourself to me. And that is what I want most. Meet with me, Lord. Open my eyes to see and know You through Your Word. Open my understanding to those things You want to show me, and teach me truth that will set me free."

We have His assurance that He will abundantly respond to our desire. In fact, to be more accurate, *He* is actively seeking intimacy *with us*, and He desires *our* response. The Lord Jesus says:

> Here I am! I stand at the door and knock. If anyone hears My voice and opens the door, I will go in and eat with him, and he with Me (Revelation 3:20).

We are not dealing with a reluctant God whose arm we must twist in order to get His attention; *He earnestly desires us.* He wants to pour out to us life in abundance and joy beyond measure. The possession of God's Word is an unspeakable blessing. What a tragedy it is for someone to see Bible study as a "discipline," a drudgery, and an unrewarding duty that we have to perform!

Second, *study dependently*. I will not belabor this point, since I have made it several times in other chapters. Briefly, we must study God's Word with the firm conviction that we cannot understand spiritual truth on our own. Spiritual understanding is something that must be revealed by the Holy Spirit (1 Corinthians 2:9-16). Only by His power can you understand—

> how wide and long and high and deep is the love of Christ, and to know this love that surpasses knowledge—that you may be filled to the measure of all the fullness of God (Ephesians 3:18,19).

Anybody, including the lost, can learn *theology*—that is, what the Bible *says*. But if we truly want to know *God* and to understand what the Bible *means*, we must approach the Word in total dependence upon the Lord to reveal Himself and His truth that sets us free. Remember that "God opposes the proud but gives grace to the humble" (James 4:6).

Third, *read the Bible normally, and in large contexts*. Imagine that you and I are friends, and while on a long trip overseas you write me a long letter. After many months away, you arrive home and find me waiting for you at the airport. I look terribly confused and worried, as if I had been in that condition for a long time. After greeting me, you ask me why I seem so distressed. "It's this letter you wrote me," I say. "I've gone practically crazy trying to understand what you're talking about, but it's a total mystery to me." I pull out of my pocket several pages of the tattered letter.

You are genuinely puzzled, not aware of anything in your letter was that confusing. "What in my letter don't you understand?" you ask.

"It's this part on page 4," I answer. As I show you the letter, you can see that the page is covered with lines, notes, and different-colored highlights. I continue explaining, "I've been trying to figure out this sentence here, but it doesn't make any sense! I've looked up all the words in the dictionary and written out the optional definitions. I consulted English grammar books, and I diagrammed the sentence. I've asked all my friends, and even made an appointment with my old English teacher to ask her opinion. But nobody can really satisfy me. I've been sitting on pins and needles, waiting to ask you personally."

You give me a hard look and ask me slowly, "Bob, that sentence is on page 4. Did you read the rest of the letter?"

"No," I answer. "I've just been studying this sentence!"

What would you think of me? You would think I was a little strange, to say the least. Nobody would read a letter that way. When you read a letter, you start at the beginning and read until you get to the end. You cannot take a sentence and interpret it out in the thin air. It has no meaning apart from its total context. A sentence needs all the other words, sentences, and paragraphs that surround it to make up the entire message.

But how do people often read their Bibles? They start with chapter 5, paragraph 2, verse 3—then wonder why they can't make sense out of God's Word! Yes, the Bible is unique in its origin and inspiration, but it is constructed in the same way as all other written works. It too is made up of words, sentences, and paragraphs organized according to the ordinary rules of grammar. When you read, for example, Hebrews chapter 9, the writer assumes that you have read and followed his thoughts for the first eight chapters. Though there are difficult portions of Scripture, people will find most of the questions they raise about verses of the Bible answered *if they will only keep reading.*

There is certainly a place for methods such as word studies or topical studies; they can be enjoyable and profitable. But these should be *supplementary* methods, not our main type of study, or we will not have a balanced and full understanding of the Scriptures.

When I was a new Christian there were many things I didn't understand, but I didn't let that stop me. I didn't expect God to teach me everything in one day! I also remembered that Jesus told His disciples on the night before His death:

> I have much more to say to you, more than you can now bear. But when He, the Spirit of truth, comes, He will guide you into all truth (John 16:12,13).

If the men with whom Jesus walked for three years still could not "bear" or comprehend all His teaching, who was I to think I could get it all instantly? So whenever I came across a hard verse or passage I simply put a checkmark by it with the prayer, "Lord, this must be one of those things I'm not ready for. But You know that, whenever You decide, I'm here to learn what it means." And I would continue reading. In most cases a few chapters or perhaps a few books later in the New Testament I would find the answer. That was always a thrill, as I would say, "Aha! There it is!" and write in my Bible the cross-reference from the question to the answer. Over time, as I kept reading, God filled out my understanding of biblical truth, while I enjoyed spending time with my Lord. When you come across hard passages, remember this simple rule: Never interpret obvious passages in the light of obscure ones; always intepret obscure passages in the light of the obvious ones. So when in doubt, keep reading!

A fourth point that I believe is crucial, especially for people who are just beginning to study the Scriptures, is to *emphasize the New Testament in your study*. This is commonly misunderstood. "Are you saying that the Old Testament is not God's Word?" people ask. "You're throwing out half the Bible!" others accuse. No, let me say directly: All of the Bible—Old and New Testaments—is the Word of God. "All Scripture is God-breathed and is useful for teaching, rebuking, correcting and training in righteousness" (2 Timothy 3:16). However, we live in the age of the New Covenant, and it is essential that we clearly understand the covenant *under which we actually live*. Only when you have gotten a firm handle on the provisions of the New Covenant are you able to properly interpret and apply the Old Covenant.

For many centuries, world history has been divided into events that occurred before the birth of Christ (B.C.) and those that occurred afterward (A.D.). I have often thought that this was misleading. The real dividing point of human history is not Christ's birth, but his *death*. Jesus had said, "I have not come to abolish [the Law or the Prophets] but *to fulfill them*" (Matthew 5:17), and He did this when He died for the sins of the world. He fulfilled the law. But at His last supper with the disciples, He also said, "This cup is the new covenant in My blood" (1 Corinthians 11:25). Through the cross the Old Covenant was fulfilled and the New Covenant was put into effect. That's why *the cross is the real dividing point of history*.

It is like a man's last will and testament. If my father wrote out his will, would I receive my inheritance? Not right away:

> In the case of a will, it is necessary to prove the death of the one who made it, because a will is in force only when somebody has died; it never takes effect while the one who made it is living (Hebrews 9:16,17).

Not only must the writer die, but then it is only his *last* will that counts. It wouldn't matter if my father had written a dozen other wills over his lifetime. The one that goes into effect at his death is the *final* version. We can look at the Old and New Covenants in the same way. God did make a covenant with the nation of Israel, but He later promised a new covenant to come. Therefore, which one is "legal" for us today? The last will, the one we call the *New* Covenant. Reading old versions of my father's will might be enjoyable and give me insights into his life at various times in the past, but none of those wills are binding today. In the same way, reading the Old Testament can give me insight into the way God dealt with men at different times in history, but the law is no longer binding. I go to the New Testament to learn about living in this day and age.

Last, but not least, *major on the majors and minor on the minors*. It sounds strange, but not all of the tangents into which Christians stray away from Christ are unbiblical. We can actually get off on *biblical* truth. It is absolutely imperative that we not only teach the Bible, but that we teach *biblical truths according to the proper emphases given to them in the Scriptures.*

As a counselor, for example, I have faced many hundreds of individuals who are dealing with serious personal problems and tragedies. In all that experience I have never had someone say to me, "Bob, my husband has just died, and I'm just heartbroken. Tell me: What do you think is my spiritual gift?" Nobody has ever said to me, "Bob, I just lost my job, and my wife and I are going through terrible marital problems. Tell me,

I've just got to know: What does '666' signify in the book of Revelation?" Those subjects are certainly in the Bible, but they are not "majors."

Do you know what someone having serious problems wants to know? He's crying out, "Is there really a God out there? A God who really loves me, who knows what's going on in my life, who cares, and who can do something for me?" That's what you want to know when real life smacks you in the face.

So what are the "majors" in the Word of God? *Jesus Christ.* Knowing Him in a personal way. Learning what it means that He not only laid down His life *for* you, but that He now lives *in* you, and learning how to let Him live out that life *through* you. Learning how to live a life of dependency on Christ's love for us, and concentrating on the priority left to us by the Lord:

> A new command I give you: Love one another. As I have loved you, so you must love one another. By this all men will know that you are My disciples, if you love one another (John 13:34,35).

God has told us in no uncertain terms what His highest priority is. He did not say that "all men will know you are My disciples by your bumper stickers," nor that "all men will know you are My disciples by your knowledge of prophecy." Paul warned pointedly that we can speak with the tongues of men and angels, know all mysteries and have all knowledge, have mountain-moving faith, and give away all that we own or even our own lives—but have it all be worthless to God: If we have not love, we gain nothing (1 Corinthians 13:1-3). When John wanted to sum up the commandments of God, he put it this way: "This is His command: to believe in the name of His Son,

Jesus Christ, and to love one another as He commanded us" (1 John 3:23).

It never ceases to amaze me how we can major on a hundred minor issues of the Scriptures while ignoring the things which are God's highest priorities. We still have many tendencies like the Pharisees, who would "strain out a gnat but swallow a camel" (Matthew 23:24). On the other hand, if we will give ourselves to the study of and concentration on God's greatest directives, we will find that He teaches us the lesser issues as well—and our understanding will be balanced according to the biblical pattern.

Another way people get off track is by taking a biblical truth and *misusing* it. We have already seen this in our discussion of the proper use of the law. Paul said, "We know that the law is good if one uses it properly" (1 Timothy 1:8). The law is properly used to show a man his need so that he will turn to Jesus Christ for salvation. It is improperly used when it is used to try to live the Christian life.

Many other subjects are also commonly misused. Instead of giving us an appreciation for our own and other people's roles in the body of Christ, spiritual gifts can be misused to create competition and generate spiritual pride. Instead of giving us a more secure hope and enabling us to correctly make priority decisions in our present lives, the study of prophecy can become the ultimate experience of ear-tickling and ego-stroking.

Therefore, this is what it means to "major on the majors and minor on the minors": Since the Bible gives great emphasis and volume to teaching the Person and work of Jesus Christ, the correct purposes and distinctions between law and grace, walking by faith in the living Christ, and loving one another just as He loved us, those are the things I want to emphasize in my study and thought. Other scriptural issues that are of minor importance merit a minor amount of my study time and concentration.

If you will go into God's Word applying these tips—seeking to meet with the Person of Christ, studying dependently, reading in order and in large contexts, emphasizing the New Testament, and majoring on the majors—you will find that the Bible is not nearly the mystery book you had thought. You will find that being personally taught by God is the most exciting experience on earth, and nobody will have to figure out a way to motivate you to do your Bible study. As Jesus said, "Man does not live on bread alone, but on every word that comes from the mouth of God" (Matthew 4:4). No one has to convince me to be "disciplined" and eat my dinner every evening. Eating dinner is a pleasure! In the same way, when you've experienced having your *spiritual* dinner abundantly supplied by God through His Word, no one will have to force you to eat spiritually either.

Finally, let me add a few words about teachers, commentaries, and other study helps. Because of my strong push for Christians to dig into their own Bibles and study for themselves, people sometimes ask, "Are you saying that we shouldn't learn from teachers or from commentaries?" If you stop and think, that would be a pretty ridiculous position for someone who is a Bible teacher to take! However, even though we can benefit from teachers, that is not the same thing as saying that we should be totally *dependent* upon human teachers for our understanding of God's truth.

The Christian life is lived *individually*, and only our individual faith in and personal knowledge of Christ will carry us when real life sends the waves of trials and tribulations crashing in. Secondly, no human teacher, no matter how gifted, is infallible. That is why I continually tell the listeners of "People to People": "Don't take what I'm saying as total truth. Go to the Bible and check out my teaching, and see if it agrees with the Word of God." Thirdly, to completely depend upon what other Christians have learned about the truth of God, whether through teachers or their commentaries, is to be robbed of one of the greatest privileges and joys of a child of God, which is to be personally taught by our Father in heaven. To me, it would be like eating prechewed and digested food. I could go totally to commentaries and to what other gifted Christians have learned about God in a predigested form, but what a waste! What a loss it would be to me to miss the joy of having the Holy Spirit show me the depths and meaning of the Word! So while I may benefit from other people's insights and experiences, I don't ever want those resources to become *substitutes* for my personal study.

Don't be intimidated by the Bible. It is full of *good news* about God, and what He has done and will do for you in Christ! Remember that *the same Holy Spirit who inspired men to write the Scriptures lives in you*, and will illumine your mind to understand the truth of God as you approach His Word as a humble, teachable child.

As you fill your mind with the Word of God and put it into practice—becoming a doer of the Word and not merely a hearer (James 1:22)—God will be developing you into a man or woman of *conviction*.

Personal convictions formed from biblical truth are the backbone of our lives. They give our lives strength and structure, much like your skeleton does for your body. Biblical convictions can also be compared to the policy manual of a business organization. The purpose of a policy manual is to define the identity, purposes, and guidelines of a company *in order to eliminate needless decision-making*. A policy manual enables the top management of a company to concentrate on the most important aspect of their jobs—to oversee the big picture of the organization, and to provide leadership—without becoming bogged down in routine and trivial decisions, and without having the various departments go in 14 different directions. In other words, routine decisions are made in advance. Departments have guidelines as they are performing their jobs; they know what they can and cannot do, because the purposes and "out-of-bounds markers" are clearly stated. And the workers have a clearcut understanding of "who we are at XYZ Inc., what we believe in, and what we are trying to accomplish." Apart from clearly defined policies, even a small company would be chaos.

I believe that many Christians suffer continual chaos in their personal lives and in daily decision-making for this very reason: They have no *personal* "policy manual," which are those firmly held, biblical convictions. We also need to know "who I am as a child of God, what I believe in, and why I am here." God's Word gives us the truth in all these areas. Those convictions also perform the role of eliminating routine decision-making. I don't wonder or lose sleep over whether I should do certain things or go certain places. God's Word has already spoken on them, and I have accepted the Bible as absolute truth. Therefore I am free to concentrate on "setting my heart on things above" (Colossians 3:1-3) and on "serving one another in love" (Galatians 5:13). This is where we discover the truth of the Scripture which says, "God did not give us a spirit of timidity, but a spirit of power, of love and of self-discipline" (2 Timothy 1:7).

These are just some of the ramifications of following Paul's exhortation: "Do not conform any longer to the pattern of this world, but be transformed by the renewing of your mind" (Romans 12:2). This will happen as we give our minds to God to be renewed according to truth. When we "abide in His Word," we discover that truth does indeed set us free!

TWELVE

❧❧

Abundant Life Today

As part of the "People to People" ministry, we have written a number of evangelistic and Bible study materials, which have gone all over the globe. Occasionally we hear back from people who have used them. There was a period a few years ago when we heard from several young people in a remote area of Nigeria. Apparently a missionary was using our "Born Free" evangelistic booklet and our "Personal Growth Series" Bible study booklets, and was encouraging his students to write to us.

There was one short note I will never forget. In halting and misspelled English it said:

Deer Bob George. That is the most sweetums name under heven. Angles and sky rejois at yor most Christan life. Will you send me a watch?

That letter gave me one of the biggest laughs I've ever had, and it reminded me of how I have seen many Christians approach the subject of prayer. Too many of us view prayer as simply a way to "get things done"—as flattery in order to get

195

something we want—rather than as communication with God as a result of our personal relationship.

Often some of the greatest hindrances we face come from our own teaching methods. In an effort to make everything easily applicable, we come up with "formulas" and "handles" for biblical truth. Sermons become "three points and a poem," where the points always start with the same letter and have a clever rhythm. Commentators strain to devise catchy outlines for books of the Bible, and force the written text to fit into their confines. We try to reduce the Christian life to a series of "steps," and we search the Scriptures not to allow them to speak for themselves but to find proof-texts to justify our "ten steps to become spiritual." As a result, people are more concerned with remembering a teacher's points than they are in personally encountering God through His Word.

This is what has happened to prayer for many people. A common memory device for the "steps to prayer" has been ACTS: Adoration, Confession, Thanksgiving, Supplication (making requests). People have searched the biblical record of individuals' prayers through the centuries, have noticed that these elements are commonly found, and have invented a formula that we must supposedly follow to approach God in order to get what we want from Him.

In this approach God can be perceived more as a vending machine than as a Person! I put in my quarter of faith, pull the knob in order to get what I want, and out it comes. You can tell that people think like this by the way in which they talk about prayer, whether answered or unanswered. They talk about their "prayer life" and "how to pray," and proudly recount the spectacular answers they have received, "which you can receive too if you will pray like me." When they *don't* receive what they ask for, the question becomes, "What did I do wrong?" They call in a "prayer warrior" for advice on their technique, just as you would call in a repairman if your machine were not working properly.

Let's say that my son, Bobby, during his teenage years approached me this way: "Dad, have I told you lately what a great dad you are? I mean, you're such a great provider, and you're the best dad in the world" (thinking to himself, "Let's see, that's adoration. Next is confession.") "Dad, I have to confess, I haven't been totally good today. I was supposed to cut the grass, but I didn't. I'm sorry, and I'll do it tomorrow" (thinking, "Okay, that's confession. What's next? Oh, yeah, thanksgiving.") "Dad, I really want to thank you for all you do for us. Thanks for the new clothes you let me buy the other day. I really appreciate it" (thinking, "Well, that should do it. Here we go.") "Dad, can I have the car tonight?"

How would you react if your child approached you this way? I know what *I* would say: "What is this con job? If you want to use the car, why don't you just ask me, instead of going through all this other fake routine?" If no human parent would want to be approached this way (and certainly is not stupid enough to fall for it), why do we think this is what God wants?

Secondly, what kind of *relationship* could exist between a parent and child when this is their form of communication? There is no *personal interaction* at all! The parent just sits passively, waiting for the child to go through the proper ritual. The child is only interested in getting what he wants, and will go through whatever formula it takes to get it. There would be no living relationship at all under these conditions.

What is prayer? It is talking with God. It is intelligent, personal communication with our heavenly Father whom we love and who loves us. The purpose for which Jesus Christ redeemed us is to make this personal relationship possible. As mind-boggling as it may seem, God earnestly desires an intimate relationship with us, and He wants to give of His best— which is *Himself*—to us! I can hardly imagine a worse tragedy in the life of a Christian than for him to go through this life— being forgiven, justified, alive in Christ, and an heir to an eternal inheritance—without discovering the incredible joys of *knowing Him.*

We have even made the phrase "to pray in Jesus' name" into a formula. To many people it is just something to tack on the end of their prayers, like "Roger. Over and out." But that phrase is actually the source of our confidence in speaking to our Father, and it expresses a vital attitude. It is the expression of our knowledge that we have no righteousness of our own in which to approach a holy God, but that Jesus Christ has given us His righteousness. Therefore, *"In Him and though faith in Him we may approach God with freedom and confidence"* (Ephesians 3:12). That is the promise we are claiming when we pray in Jesus' name.

We have misused the prayer that Jesus gave to His disciples, the one we call "the Lord's Prayer." Jesus said:

> When you pray, do not keep on babbling like pagans, for they think they will be heard because of their many words. Do not be like them, for your Father knows what you need before you ask Him. This then is how you should pray . . . (Matthew 6:7-9).

Jesus said, "Don't pray like the pagans do," who mindlessly repeat prayers over and over and over again. "Instead," He said, "pray along these lines . . ." and He gave an example. But what have we done? We have taken the prayer that Jesus gave as an example ("along these lines") and prayed it over and over and over again, just like the pagans do! As we have done so often, we have taken an example and made it into a formula.

"Tell me how and when to pray," people ask. "Should I pray on my knees, sitting, or standing? Should I do it during other activities, or should I go away in private? Should I pray out loud or silently? Should I pray persistently about something, or should I ask God just once and trust Him to answer it?"

My answer to all these questions is, "Yes! All of the above! *There are no rigid rules.* Your own heart's desire and the overflow of your individual relationship with the Lord will guide you, and you don't have to fit into the precise pattern of any other man or woman. God loves you. Talk to Him. Tell Him what you feel, tell Him about your gratitude for what He has done in your life, tell Him your needs, ask Him to fulfill your heart's desires. What He wants most *from* you is *you.* He wants you to grow to know Him, to love Him, and to allow Him to have free access to your mind and body so that He can live through you."

I often think of the relationship I had with my dad. He was very active in politics in Indiana, and loved to discuss issues. He was firmly conservative, and naturally passed on his political philosophies to me. As I got old enough to grasp those ideas, Dad and I used to spend hours discussing political philosophies and issues. I think those were some of the most enjoyable times we spent together. The point I am making is this: I don't think I had any political understanding or held any views that my father had not taught me. He had thought them through years before. I was merely talking back to him what he had for years been saying to me. The enjoyment we shared in those discussions was not from coming up with novel ideas. It was from the meeting of our minds as we talked. I have come to see prayer in much the same light.

I like to remind people, "You have two ears and one mouth for a reason: so that you will do twice as much listening as talking." And I believe this applies to prayer, as well as to human relationships. Where do I learn truth about the God I am praying to? Through the written Word, the Scriptures. Apart from the witness of the Bible, I don't know if I have true knowledge of God or if I'm praying to a god of my own imagination. That is where the "listening" comes in. My prayer needs to be inspired by *God speaking to me*, which He does through His written Word. Then I pray God's Word back to Him—not in a formula, but as it relates to my personal life, heartaches, needs, and aspirations. As His child I maintain a teachable, responsive attitude, and I find that the Lord teaches me. He shows me His objective truth in the Bible, then He allows me to test it in order to see its real meaning. These experiences progressively deepen my confidence in the reliability of His Word, and increase my appreciation for His gentleness, faithfulness, mercy, kindness, and love.

If there is one verse that exemplifies what prayer has become in my life, it is one of the shortest verses in the Bible, 1 Thessalonians 5:17: *"Pray continually."* Obviously, if prayer were only a religious ritual, in which you had to drop to your knees, close your eyes, and fold your hands, there would be no way in the world to apply this verse. But when you see prayer as your communication with a loving and attentive heavenly Father who lives in you through the Holy Spirit, you can apply it. You can have an attitude of responsiveness, dependency, and availability to God every waking hour, and be actively speaking to Him whenever your heart is moved. There is tremendous joy and fulfillment in experiencing the reality of which Paul said, "To me, to live is Christ" (Philippians 1:21). It is those who have begun to experience this fact who are able to truthfully hold to the second half of the verse: "and to die is gain."

It is because of our real oneness with Christ, we in Him and He in us, that another error of religion is shot out of the water: the division between "spiritual" and "secular." According to the common mindset, spiritual activities are things such as going to church, reading your Bible, praying, giving money, singing hymns, and attending fellowship groups. In other words, only those activities which are overtly "religious" count as "spiritual"—and therefore of worth to God. Everything else, including going to work, recreation, household chores, and family activities, count as "secular"—and are therefore of little worth in God's eyes. This is an error that must be corrected if we are going to discover and enjoy Christ living His life through us and continue growing in grace.

Jesus had a fascinating conversation one day with a Samaritan woman, recorded in John 4:4-26. In the course of the conversation the woman mentioned the religious controversy of the time over the proper place of worship. "Our fathers [the Samaritans] worshiped on this mountain, but you Jews claim that the place where we must worship is in Jerusalem" (John 4:20). In His reply, Jesus affirms that the Jews were indeed the correct party in the controversy: "You Samaritans worship what you do not know; we worship what we do know, for salvation is from the Jews" (John 4:22).

Previously God had mandated the times and place of worship. Sabbath days, festivals, feasts, Sabbatical years, and so forth were not optional. God levied severe judgments on Israel for their failure to observe these things. Also, the place of worship was not optional. God said that sacrifices could be offered nowhere but at the proper, central place of meeting, and only through the Levitical priesthood. He said that anyone who offered sacrifices elsewhere "must be cut off from his people" (Leviticus 17:8,9). The Mosaic law was God-given, and it was specific. However, in His conversation with the Samaritan woman, Jesus revealed a major change to come. His answer was earthshaking in its impact:

> Believe me, woman, a time is coming when you will worship the Father neither on this mountain *nor in Jerusalem.* . . . A time is coming and has now come when the true worshipers will worship the Father in spirit and truth, for they are the kind of worshipers the Father seeks. *God is spirit, and His worshipers must worship in spirit and in truth* (John 4:21,23,24).

Jesus was pointing ahead to a time when the worship of the true God would no longer be tied to a particular time or place. He later went to the cross where He fulfilled the Old Covenant, bringing it to an end. At the same cross He ratified a New Covenant through His blood. God no longer lives in a temple of stone, mortar, and wood. *God's temple is now His people!* "Don't you know that you yourselves are God's temple and that God's Spirit lives in you?" Paul asked the Corinthians (1 Corinthians 3:16). He exhorted them again in 1 Corinthians 6:19,20:

> Do you not know that your body is a temple of the Holy Spirit, who is in you, whom you have received from God? You are not your own; you were bought with a price. Therefore honor God with your body.

If Christ lives in His people, then the real "church" is not that building "at the corner of 'walk' and 'don't walk.'" No *building* is the church! *God's people are the church!* Therefore, where is the church on Sunday morning? It is meeting in buildings all over the city, wherever there are gatherings of people who are born again in Jesus Christ. Where is the church on *Monday* morning? It is in neighborhoods, schools, business buildings, and doctors' offices. The church—that is, *God's people*—are scattered in the highways and byways of life. And those people are just as much individual temples of God in business offices and those other places as they were in the church's building on Sunday.

Spirituality is determined not by the *type* of activity, but by who is the *source* of the activity. Christ lives in me. If I have presented myself to Him for His use, then anything I am doing can be called "spiritual," whether it is cutting the grass, doing laundry, talking with friends, or taking my son to a ball game! I can "pray continually," and enjoy my relationship with the Lord *wherever I am.*

It is clearly God's will that we work and provide for ourselves, if we are able, as well as to "have something to share with those in need" (Ephesians 4:28). All those hours and the mental energy that we spend in our occupation are not "wasted time" in God's eyes. Instead, they serve as opportunities for us to walk in an intimate relationship with Him, to see His faithfulness to meet our needs, and to see Him use us to shed light on a world of darkness. In other words, you can be growing in grace on the job just as much as in a Bible study.

I once had the opportunity to lead the chapel service for the ladies' professional tennis tour. I found that many of those Christian athletes felt the same discouragement in regard to their occupation that many Christian businessmen and women do. I asked them, "Do you think that people you meet around the world might also need to know Christ?" Clearly, the answer was yes. "Then do you think God needs Christians in the sphere of women's professional tennis, just as He needs Christians in businesses, schools, and neigborhoods?" Again, the answer was yes. "Then rejoice in the ability and opportunity God has given you! Practice hard, and play hard, realizing that Christ lives in you, and that He will use you in your particular sphere of influence in a unique way. Make yourself available to Him as you travel around the world. Your profession will open doors to reaching people with the gospel whom many of us will never meet. If you are presenting yourself to your heavenly Father as a 'living sacrifice,' then Christ will be living through you even on a tennis court."

Seeing yourself as a "temple of the Holy Spirit" will also transform the way you look at other Christians and relate to them within the body of Christ. As Christ more and more lives His life in and through you, you will feel an increasing desire to seek out and enjoy meeting with other people who share the same life. You will find deep pleasure in the true fellowship of like-minded believers as you focus together on Jesus Christ and His Word.

Because of the deep human need for fellowship with others, we can easily be led to look in the wrong places. As strange as it may sound, one of the erroneous ways in which we can try to achieve fellowship with other people is by making fellowship our specific aim. That is not how it happens. You do not experience the deepest and most abiding fellowship by concentrating on fellowship. *You experience true and profound Christian fellowship through a common concentration on Jesus Christ.*

Think of it this way: What if you had the task of tuning 100 pianos together? If you tried to tune them by comparing them and adjusting them to one another, you would never be able to accomplish it. *But if you will tune them all to the same tuning fork, they will automatically be in tune with one another!* In exactly the same way, when we concentrate on one another and try to come to like minds and hearts, we find nothing but discord. However, when we concentrate on Jesus Christ, on what He has done for us, on His life in us, and on the spiritual realities we share, we find that we are truly "one in the Lord." But what are those things we share? Ephesians 4:4-6 says:

> There is one body and one Spirit—just as you were called to one hope when you were called—one Lord, one faith, one baptism; one God and Father of all, who is over all and through all and in all.

It is on the basis of these things, which are objectively true, that we are exhorted:

> With all humility and gentleness, with patience, showing forbearance to one another in love, being diligent to preserve the unity of the Spirit in the bond of peace (Ephesians 4:2,3 NASB).

Our role is not to *create* our unity in Christ, but to *preserve* it! We discover our oneness in Christ through concentration on Him, and we preserve that unity by viewing and serving one another as fellow members of one body in Christ.

"Lone Ranger Christianity" is not God's plan. We are not sufficient in and of ourselves. We need one another. "In Christ we who are many form one body, and each member belongs to all the others" (Romans 12:5). None of us has all the gifts of the Holy Spirit. Therefore we not only need to serve the other members of the body through our own gifts, but we also need them to be serving us. That is why there are no "stars" or "big deals" in the Christian faith. I call myself a "spiritual hamburger joint." Through the teaching gift God has given me, I do my best to give people good "hamburgers." However, you cannot live on hamburgers alone! You need a balanced diet, and that's where the whole body of Christ comes in.

The Christian life is *Christ*. It is knowing Him and walking in Him in a trust relationship which touches *every* aspect of life in the world. Jesus Christ laid down His life *for* us, in order to give His life *to* us, in order to live His life *through* us. If we will give ourselves to Him in the same attitude of dependency that He exemplified in His walk with His Father, we will discover the exciting experience of watching Him use us in our everyday lives. Growing in grace is not something we do only in Bible studies, prayer time, or church services. The Christian life is not a subject to be learned; it is a life to be lived! All day every day is an opportunity to grow in grace and in the knowledge of our Lord and Savior Jesus Christ.

THIRTEEN

Marks
of Growth

I was once conducting a seminar in a federal prison in Texas. With me on the trip were several volunteers to assist in counseling the inmates, including one named David. David had been a believer for only about two years, but God's love had transformed his life. The cynical and hard construction-company owner I knew previously had remarkably grown in grace. David had become a softhearted, friendly, and giving man under the influence of Jesus Christ. He was very excited and was enjoying working with the inmates at the conference, when he had an unexpected and dramatic encounter.

It was during one of my final lectures, where I was discussing the need to extend the same forgiveness that we have received from God to other people. David thought that was great, and was cheering me on in his heart. "Yeah! Go, Bob!" he was thinking. "I sure hope all these prisoners are listening, because *they sure need this!*"

David was in that frame of mind, grinning and looking around to see if people were listening, when suddenly *he turned and saw the face of the man whom he hated more than any man on earth.* Several years before David became a believer, this man had done some things to hurt him severely, both personally and professionally. In fact, David's hatred and desire for revenge at that time were so intense that, as he later told me, "The only thing that kept me from hiring a hit man to kill him was the fear of getting caught!"

Now here they were: This man was an inmate in a prison, and David was a Christian who had come to work with prisoners. David had not yet been noticed, and he knew he had to make a quick decision. The struggle in his heart was incredible. Seeing that man for the first time in years had brought back all those hateful emotions in an instant—but David was now a new man. Jesus Christ had come into him, and had done tremendous things in his life; that was undeniable. But the memories and reactions of the flesh were still there. "I knew what God's Word said about forgiving one another," he says, "but I wasn't ready for anything like this! Jesus' command to 'love your enemies' sounds like a beautiful sentiment until you actually have an enemy! What I wanted more than anything in the world was a way out of that room!"

But God was living in David, and was reasoning with him according to truth. "Even though I could look back at what this man had done to me," he says, "I could now look back and see where I wasn't lily-white, either! The Lord had to do some serious forgiving in my life to make me acceptable to Him. Frankly, I couldn't see that there was very much difference between me and this other guy if you looked at us from God's perspective."

The war of emotions continued within David's heart, until I stopped speaking and announced a break. It was time to decide. A lot of David's feelings were still screaming about the old offenses, but God's love was also speaking to him. He decided to do what God said. "I walked over and stood before him," David says, "and you should have seen his reaction! He nearly jumped out of his skin when he saw me. I think he expected me to slug him. Instead, I extended my hand and said, 'I hope you're listening to these messages, because Bob is right. Jesus Christ has changed my life, and He can change yours, too.'"

The man could hardly talk for a minute. Then he shook David's hand and said slowly, "If I didn't have a reason to listen before, I sure do now!"

David will testify today that those old resentments are totally gone. The old hatreds have dissipated, and he now feels a genuine compassion for a man that he once could have willingly killed. How do you explain it? It is supernatural. Only those who have first *received* the love and grace of God can go on and become willing servants and "ministers of reconciliation" (2 Corinthians 5:18), even to bitter enemies! The Bible says, "We love because He first loved us" (1 John 4:19). The power of God is unleashed in human relationships when the message of His unconditional love and acceptance in Jesus Christ is proclaimed.

In 2 Corinthians 5:14,15 Paul describes the dominating motivation and response of the Christian life as a person grows in grace. The passage reads:

> The love of Christ controls us, having concluded this, that one died for all, therefore all died; and He died for all that they who live should no longer live for themselves, but for Him who died and rose again on their behalf (NASB).

In other words, as we grow in our knowledge of the love of God and in appreciation for what Jesus Christ has done for us, His love begins to control us—not in the sense of making us robots or forcing us against our will, but stirring up in us the desire to give ourselves back to Him: "that they who live should no longer live for themselves, but for Him." Paul is here expressing the same thought as in Romans 12:1, which we have considered several times in this book.

The very next thing Paul mentions after our giving ourselves back to "Him who died and rose again on our behalf" is *the attitude with which we look at other people.* He continues in 2 Corinthians 5:16: "Therefore from now on we recognize no man according to the flesh" (NASB). Having presented ourselves to the Lord as living sacrifices and submitting our minds to be renewed according to truth, we see people in a totally new light. We learn to look beyond outward appearances, and begin to see people as God sees them. Having been recipients of God's mercy, kindness, and love, we begin to extend those same qualities to other people.

This is the pattern that the Scriptures teach. "Love one another," Jesus told His disciples. But *how?* "*As I have loved you*" (John 13:34). "Accept one another," Paul wrote in Romans 15:7. *How?* "*Just as Christ accepted you,* in order to bring praise to God." Following this same logic, Ephesians 4:31,32 says:

> Get rid of all bitterness, rage and anger, brawling and slander, along with every form of malice. Be kind and compassionate to one another, forgiving each other, *just as in Christ God forgave you.*

It is a predictable law of human behavior that *people will give away the same kind of love, acceptance, and forgiveness that they think they are receiving from God.* In other words, if I think that God rejects me for *my* failures, I will turn around and reject you for *your* failures. People will simply not give away a higher degree of love and acceptance than they believe they are receiving from God. Therefore, you can see how necessary it is that we first *receive* God's love and forgiveness before we will ever be able to make strides in loving one another as the Bible teaches. A person who is genuinely growing in grace will be becoming more gracious toward other people.

Another unmistakable sign that the message of God's love is hitting home with people and that they are truly growing in grace is the development of an *attitude of servitude*. This is when a person is adopting the same attitude that the Lord Jesus exemplified: "The Son of Man *did not come to be served, but to serve*, and to give His life as a ransom for many" (Matthew 20:28). "You, my brothers, were called to be free," Paul tells us in Galatians 5:13. "But do not use your freedom to indulge the sinful nature; rather, *serve one another in love*." When God is at work in a person's heart, this supernatural quality can be exercised under some of the most amazing circumstances.

I will never forget visiting another city for a seminar, when three radiant young women came up to meet me. Two of the three ladies were handicapped—one on crutches and the other in a wheelchair. They introduced themselves, and we chatted awhile about the conference. Then the one on crutches, Kathryn, said with a laugh, "You know, Bob, you could never guess what the three of us have in common!" I asked her to elaborate, and she said, "Well, to begin with, all three of us tried to commit suicide by jumping! Terri (the one walking) and I both tried to kill ourselves by jumping off the bridge over the river. Margie (the one in the wheelchair) jumped off a building.

And now we have formed a ministry together to help other depressed people."

Kathryn explained further: "After my suicide attempt, I spent many years in and out of institutions. I had two nervous breakdowns, and received every type of treatment, including electroshock. But nothing ever cured me. Then Terri was introduced to me. When I heard that she had jumped off the same bridge in the same year that I did, we had an instant bond. She shared the gospel with me as well as your tapes on experiencing 'Victory Over Depression.' Finally, I began to see that the problem with me was *me*! I accepted Jesus Christ as my Savior, and I experienced a real relief and joy for the first time. Now my life is lived for Him. His Spirit lives in me, filling me with peace, joy, and hope. I'm not without troubles, or even without depression, but the difference is that now I know He's with me every step of the way. I rely on His strength, and not mine."

Kathryn and Terri became close friends and attended Bible study together. One day they met Margie, who had suffered a more crippling injury through her own suicide attempt. The three began to meet together, and the idea for the support group was born.

Kathryn explained, "Our purpose is to share our life stories with others who suffer from depression, a vicious crippler. We in the group realize that, though our situations may be different, the problems and pain of depression are the same. Our focus is Jesus Christ, because He is the answer—the only answer."

Though I have seen God do great things through the years to transform lives, the picture of these three happy, stable women amazed me. Each one had a history of years of rejection, anger, dependency, and depression. Two of them had permanent physical damage as a result of their struggles. From the world's stand-point, you would expect them to be angry and resentful for the rest of their lives. There are no more predictable characteristics of depression than anger, self-pity, and a total preoccupation with self. Yet these women were peaceful and joyful, and were looking *outward* to serve the needs of *other people!* Jesus Christ had not only healed the turmoil of their own souls, but He had transformed their hearts into tune with His: "The Son of Man did not come to be served, but to serve." Their story perfectly illustrates the truth found in 2 Corinthians 1:3,4:

> Praise be to the God and Father of our Lord Jesus Christ, the Father of compassion and the God of all comfort, who comforts us in all our troubles, so that we can comfort those in any trouble with the comfort we ourselves have received from God.

Jesus said, "In this world you will have trouble" (John 16:33), and that applies to all of us. Whatever the particular brand of trouble that comes to us we can be sure of this: We are not alone. There are many, many other people who are in the same boat. Therefore we can see good in the midst of our tribu-lations. Satan may intend them for evil, but God takes them and causes them to work together for good. One way is by using them to make us more effective and more compassionate servants.

I have found through my counseling experience that I usually have little compassion for people going through problems I have never experienced. That is when we Christians have a tendency to be "quick relief pill" counselors: We simply pop out a Bible verse or truth in answer to people's problems. We share an answer, and perhaps a true answer, but it is without heart. And people tend to reject counsel that is offered without compassion.

However, when we've been there ourselves, our heart goes out to a person in trouble. We know what it feels like, and we know how hard it is to resist the assault on our minds when we are in the midst of pressure. But at the same time we can speak with authority on the answer.

One day we received a desperate call at the office from a woman who was suicidal. Normally we have many men and women available who are fine counselors, but at this time there was no one in the office but Lori, the receptionist who answered the phone. Lori had gone through our training course just a few weeks earlier and felt totally inadequate to help the caller, but she was on the spot, since there was no one else to help. So she listened awhile as the woman poured out her story of abuse, rejection, and depression. Lori began asking questions about the caller's relationship with Christ, and shared some truths about how He can give us peace, but the caller was resistant. "Oh, I need answers that work," she moaned. "You don't understand . . ."

"No, *you* don't understand!" interrupted Lori. "*I've been there*. Just a few years ago I felt just like you. I tried all my life to be accepted, and finally came to the point where I wanted to take my own life too. But Jesus Christ is real, and He really does give you peace when you learn about His unconditional love and acceptance. I *know* that it is true, because He changed my life."

As Lori shared more about her own experience, the caller softened and listened more intently. It was obvious that Lori really did relate to her. And the way in which Lori shared the answer—authoritatively, but with compassion and understanding—won her a hearing. After almost two hours on a long-distance phone call, Lori led the caller to faith in Jesus Christ. I met this woman later, and her life is firmly on the ground. She is growing in grace today as a child of God, free from the resentments, anger, and self-pity which held her in bondage for years.

I once heard a story about a sculptor. He stood before a massive block of marble, with hammer and chisel in hand, when a visitor asked him, "What are you going to do with that ugly block of stone?" The sculptor's answer was, "I'm about to free the beautiful angel that is trapped inside."

That reminds me of the difference between our perspective and God's perspective on people and life's circumstances. We see other people, and ourselves, like the ugly block of stone. We see things only as they are now. But God, like the sculptor, sees us as we *will be*. Though the process is not always pleasurable, the trials and tribulations we encounter are God's "hammer and chisel" to shape us into the image of Christ. Through the pressures and problems we face, we learn to lean more dependently upon the Lord. As a result, we learn that His peace truly does "transcend understanding" (Philippians 4:7), because, unlike the world's peace, it is not dependent upon circumstances. Through dependency upon Christ, we come to know Him and experience His life, and we see Him use us to "serve one another in love" (Galatians 5:13). As we allow the indwelling life of Christ to dominate our lives, we increasingly take on the appearance of a servant.

Because of the deepening of this desire to "serve one another in love," we even become willing to restrict the use of our freedom when necessary, for love's sake. While we certainly never want to pervert the truth of God's grace in the face of legalism, it is a mark of increasing maturity to determine "not

to put any stumbling block or obstacle in your brother's way"
(Romans 14:13). As Paul explains:

> We who are strong ought to bear with the failings of the
> weak and not to please ourselves. Each of us should please
> his neighbor for his good, to build him up (Romans 15:1,2).

According to Paul, the mature use of freedom involves the
realization that serving others for their good is more important
than fulfilling my own desires. "Though I am free and belong
to no man," he said, "I make myself a slave to everyone, to win
as many as possible" (1 Corinthians 9:19). Let's take a simple
example: Let's say I want to share the gospel with my neighbor,
who is forbidden to eat pork because of his Jewish religion.
What kind of hearing do you think I would receive if I were to
invite him over for a nice dinner of baked ham? None. The
dinner itself, not to mention my own insensitivity, would be so
offensive that he would turn me off before I ever got started.

A person with a misunderstanding of the grace of God may
say, "But the Bible says that all foods are allowed now. You
shouldn't compromise on your freedom. We are no longer
under the Old Testament dietary laws." That is irrelevant. The
issue is not *law*—what I *can or cannot eat*. The issue is *my use of
freedom*: whether my use of freedom is governed by *love*
("pleasing my neighbor for *his* good"), or whether in my immaturity I care more about my own wants than about leading
someone to Christ. If we really care about people, and the love
of Christ is determining our decisions, we will make the same
decision as Paul: "We put no stumbling block in anyone's path,
so that our ministry will not be discredited" (2 Corinthians
6:3). Am I interested in serving others in love, or in serving
myself? *That* is the issue!

You can see from this example why our freedom in Christ is foundational to growing in grace. Under law, you are told exactly what to do and when; you never have to think for yourself or learn to make mature choices. Under the freedom of grace, however, we learn to make decisions motivated by the love of Christ and out of love for other people. Law wants to *manage* people, to keep them in line; but people grow in maturity only under grace, where they learn to make decisions from proper motivations.

These are some of the marks of the grace of God in action. You see a person exhibiting a genuine and realistic kind of love—not acting under compulsion, nor becoming a "great pretender." Instead it is love that comes from within as a result of basking in the love and grace of Jesus Christ. It is the fruit of abiding in Him in a personal relationship. It is the freedom that comes from knowing the truth, which we learn by abiding in His objective Word. Growing in grace is the result of stepping out in dependency on God and His Word, sustained by our hope in His faithfulness and motivated by the love which He has lavished upon us.

Apart from the message of God's love and grace, Christianity becomes a kind of religious high-jump competition. Even if you make the jump, you can never rest. Immediately the bar is raised another notch. Eventually the bar is raised to a level you can't jump over. You give it all you've got but find it's not enough. That's when you are tempted to give up, thinking, "I am a failure as a Christian."

The Lord never intended us to burn out "giving it all we've got." We are called to a shared life with Him. He is the One who said:

Come to Me, all you who are weary and burdened, and I will give you rest. Take My yoke upon you and learn from Me, for I am gentle and humble in heart, and you will find rest for your souls. For My yoke is easy and My burden is light (Matthew 11:28-30).

Many people today have never seen a yoke. Here's my up-to-date version of His promise: Imagine yourself in a car with two sets of driving controls. Two steering wheels, two gas pedals, two brakes, and so forth. You are in one seat, and the Lord is in the other. He says to you, "My child, I have great plans for you. I will reveal Myself to you, shower you with My love and acceptance, set you free by renewing your mind with My truth, and conform you to My image as we go through life together. All you have to do is enjoy the ride and let Me drive. But notice that before you is your own set of driving controls. You have the capability of grabbing the steering wheel and taking things into your own hands. Only one of us can drive at a time, and the choice is yours. If you take control, I will take My hands off. I promise that, whatever you choose, I will never leave you nor forsake you. If you drive off a cliff, I will be with you all the way. But isn't it far better to allow Me to drive? I love you. I have all wisdom, all power, and I am committed to your ultimate good. I ask you to trust Me, but the choice is yours."

Under the influence of error or fear we are often tempted to grab the wheel. The Lord, however, continues to be faithful. As we learn to trust Him, we find ourselves experiencing what the writer of Hebrews called the "Sabbath-rest": "There remains, then, a Sabbath-rest for the people of God; for anyone who enters God's rest also rests from his own work, just as God did from His" (Hebrews 4:9,10).

By a lake one evening Jesus told His disciples, "Let's go over to the other side" (Mark 4:35). That was the night a great storm arose, and the disciples were terrified as their small boat was tossed violently. They awakened the Lord, who immediately commanded the wind and waves to be still. He then said to them, "Why are you so afraid? Have you still no faith?" (Mark 4:40). Why the reference to their lack of faith? It's because He had said to them, "We're going to the other side." You can count on His word. If the Lord says we're going to the other side, we're going to the other side!

We are much like those disciples. The Lord has given us tremendous promises in His Word, but we still focus on the wind and waves in our lives. This same Lord is He who will fulfill the promise of Philippians 1:6: "He who began a good work in you will carry it on to completion until the day of Christ Jesus." If He said He will complete the work He began in you, you can count on it: He will complete the work He began in you! So rest in Him.

As we grow in grace, we gain a greater perspective on our lives. We no longer see ourselves as just wandering through this world. Jesus Christ lives in us! We have meaning and purpose, a race to run. And the Lord stands at the finish line with the greatest reward I can imagine: the words "Well done, good and faithful servant" (Matthew 25:21).

A lot of people, enamored by this world's "toys," seem to live as if they were on the "200-year plan." But there's no time to waste. At best we have only a few short years on this earth, and life is too short to miss the real thing! Life is too short to miss the experience of walking in a trust relationship with the living Christ, drinking in the abundant life and the love He offers us, and seeing Him use us to accomplish things of eternal worth while we are passing through this world on the way to our real home.

"I have been crucified with Christ," Paul wrote, "and I no longer live, but Christ lives in me. The life I live in the body, I live by faith in the Son of God, who loved me and gave Himself for me" (Galatians 2:20). As we continue making that same decision, to live by faith in the Son of God, who loved us and gave Himself for us, we can trust God to fulfill His promise: "He who began a good work in you will carry it on to completion until the day of Christ Jesus" (Philippians 1:6). "*God is faithful*, through whom you were called into fellowship with His Son, Jesus Christ our Lord" (1 Corinthians 1:9 NASB).

Growing in grace, our ongoing experience of "classic Christianity," is not "giving it all you've got"; it's allowing Him to give you all *He's* got! It is a vital, living relationship with a Person— the Lord Jesus Christ. Let Him drive and enjoy the ride!

A Personal Invitation...

If after reading *Growing in Grace* you realize that you have never accepted God's offer of salvation in Jesus Christ, or if you simply are not sure whether you are in Christ, I invite you to receive Him right now. John 1:12 says, "To all who received him, to those who believed in his name, he gave the right to become children of God." In Christ is total forgiveness of sins, total acceptance, and eternal life.

Salvation is a free gift that you accept by faith. You are not saved by prayer, although prayer can be a way of concretely expressing your faith in Christ. For example, here is a suggested prayer:

> Lord Jesus, I need You. Thank You for dying for the forgiveness of my sins, and for offering me Your righteousness and resurrected life. I now accept by faith Your gift of salvation. Through Your Holy Spirit, teach me about Your love and grace, and about the new life that You have given me. Begin the work of making me into the person You want me to be. Amen.

Again, there is nothing magical about praying these exact words; God is looking at the heart that trusts fully in Him.

If you have received Jesus Christ through reading *Growing in Grace*, or if your life has been impacted in other ways through the ministry of this book, or if you would like more information about our ministry, I would very much appreciate hearing from you. Please write to me, Bob George, c/o People to People, 2300 Valley View Lane, Suite 200, Dallas, TX 75234. May God bless you with a deep personal understanding and experience of His matchless love and grace!

Growing
in Grace

STUDY GUIDE

Contents

ONE

Real Life in the Real World

Peter tells us that we have been given "everything we need for life and godliness" (2 Peter 1:3). Every person who begins his Christian life begins it with everything he will ever receive. Even so, have you ever asked, "If I've been given everything, why do I continue to struggle?"

How does Paul describe the struggle he experienced in Romans 7:15,18,19?

To what does he attribute his behavior—if I do what I do not want to do—in Romans 7:17,20?

What does Peter say will war against our souls in 1 Peter 2:11?

What advice does he give regarding sinful desires?

Does Peter say these sinful desires will go away?

How does Paul describe the relationship between the flesh and the Spirit in Galatians 5:17?

What is the result of this conflict?

According to these verses, should our struggle as Christians with sin and the desires of the flesh surprise us?

In the midst of this struggle, therefore, in 2 Peter 3:18, what does Peter tell us to grow in?

A Rough-and-Tumble World

Growing in grace is not a set of steps to follow or a series of principles to master. It is more than a subject to be learned; it is a life to be lived. You can't grow in grace through books, seminars, or "quiet times," but only through a personal relationship with Jesus Christ, who teaches you truth from His Word, which you then take out into the rough-and-tumble of real life in the real world.

What does John say that we will have in this world (John 16:33)?

According to James 1:2, what can we expect to face in this life?

What do these trials test, according to James 1:3?

J.E. found out that he had terminal lung cancer. If he was to grow in grace, under what sort of circumstances would this have to happen?

Gary heard the gospel while in prison and was born again. If Gary was to grow in grace, where would that process have to take place?

If you are to grow in grace, what sort of circumstances will you have to grow in?

How Much Can We Do?

It's a rough-and-tumble world that we live in, filled with troubles, trials and sufferings. But that's where we grow—in the midst of real life. But to grow in grace we must *focus* on what God is doing in the midst of what we are doing.

In John 15:4, can a branch bear fruit by itself?

In the same way, can we bear fruit by ourselves?

Who is the true Vine, according to John 15:5?

When we abide in the Vine, what is the result in our lives?

How much can we do apart from Christ?

Could I produce a love in my heart for Bernie apart from Christ?

Whom does Hebrews 12:2 say that we are to fix our eyes on?

How does John describe Jesus, the One we fix our eyes on, in John 1:14?

How do these passages substantiate the statement "We grow in grace as we focus on what God is doing in the midst of what we are doing"?

Who Are You?

Our identity in Christ is a truth that we will find ourselves coming back to again and again as we grow in grace. This truth produces a constant standard against which we learn to measure our thinking and responses throughout all of life.

What does God's Spirit testify to our spirit that we are, according to Romans 8:16?

What else are we, if we are children of God, according to Romans 8:17?

What does Galatians 3:26 say is our identity?

How does Paul describe our identity in Ephesians 5:8?

How does he tell us to live as a result?

Will our identity as children of God ever change?

Why do you think our identity is foundational in the process of growing in grace?

Hope to Grow

For what purpose did Christ come, according to John 10:10?

What is Christ's purpose for you?

What does God promise to do in our lives, according to Romans 8:29?

In 1 Corinthians 3:6 Paul said he planted the seed and Apollos watered it. Who made it grow?

According to Philippians 1:6, what is God committed to do in your life as His child?

Can God be trusted to fulfill His promise and cause us to grow?

Whom does our hope to grow in grace come from, according to the above passages?

There is good news, a restored hope, and great encouragement in the chapters ahead. My prayer is that God will open the eyes of your heart to help you understand His love and grace toward you, so you will discover truly abundant life as you grow in His wonderful grace.

TWO

*Called
to a Person*

Many Christians have dedicated themselves to self-discipline and self-improvement, only to find that something is missing. They latch on to the latest Christian fad, hoping that maybe this could be the answer. This continuous search for something more has led thousands of Christians to say, "I've tried the Christian life, and it doesn't work."

What was Paul's fear in 2 Corinthians 11:2,3?

How can our minds be led astray from sincere and pure devotion to Christ?

How did Jesus describe the church in Ephesus in Revelation 2:2,3?

This sounds so positive, yet what did He hold against them in verse 4?

Whom did they stumble over?

According to Galatians 3:3, how were the Galatians trying to obtain their goal?

What did Paul call them as a result (Galatians 3:1)?

Who does Paul say is our life in Colossians 3:4?

When we are dependent on our own human efforts to make the Christian life work, who is missing?

The Christian life is not an *it*! The Christian life is *Christ*—a vital personal relationship with the One who laid down His life for you, so that He could give His life to you, so that He could live His life through you. He is what we have been missing in the midst of all our highly dedicated efforts!

Known by God

Christ indeed is our life. John defines eternal life as *knowing* the only true God, and Jesus Christ (John 17:3). The proof of our personal relationship is not only in our *knowing Him*, however. By definition, a relationship cannot be just one way. Just as important: *Does He know us?*

Read John 2:23-25. In verse 23, why did the people believe in His name?

Even though they believed, why did Jesus not entrust Himself to them, according to verse 24?

What does Jesus know about us, according to verse 25?

If we do not believe we are known by Christ, to whom will we turn to discover who we are?

What does a misunderstanding of this truth force us to become, according to James 1:8?

Can we understand ourselves apart from Christ, according to Romans 7:15?

What does Galatians 2:20 say has happened to us?

Who now lives in us?

Based on the fact that Christ lives in us, if we are to get to know ourselves, whom are we going to have to know?

Our calling is to Him. When we stray, we become double-minded and unstable. When we realize that Christ knows us inside and out, we can trust Him to teach us who we are and not rely on our own human efforts.

Our Calling to Him

Have you heard these statements: "I am called to preach" or "We are saved to serve"? I've talked to many people who have made these claims who are burned out. Like the Galatians, they have centered their Christian lives on their human efforts: preaching, serving, or whatever they feel their calling is.

Our primary calling is not to serve. Our calling is to Christ. In contrast to our futile efforts to live the Christian life, Jesus Christ continues to say, "Come to Me."

Whom does Jesus bid to come to Him in Matthew 11:28?

Does this describe you?

What will we find when we take upon ourselves the yoke of Jesus (Matthew 11:29,30)?

Whom does Jesus bid to come to Him in John 7:37,38?

What is the result in those who believe in Christ?

Why does Jesus say to come to Him in John 6:35?

What will be the result in our lives?

Why does Jesus say to follow Him in John 8:12?

What will be the result in our lives?

How does Jesus describe Himself in John 10:11,27-30?

What does the Good Shepherd do for the sheep?

What does the Good Shepherd give to His sheep?

How much security do we have in Him?

What are Christ's claims about Himself in John 14:6?

How do we come to the Father?

How does Jesus describe Himself in John 11:25,26, and what is the result of believing in Him?

How are we to bear fruit in our Christian lives, according to John 15:5?

A Bunch of Sheepdogs

My wife described our ministry like this: "We're just a bunch of sheepdogs trying to herd the sheep back to the Shepherd." Whatever the need of the human heart, Christ offers Himself as the solution. Our role and the role of this book is to point you to Him.

Whom are we to fix our eyes on, according to Hebrews 12:2?

Do you think Satan cares what our eyes are on, as long as they are not on Christ?

In light of the above verse, explain the statement "Anything that is not centered on the living Christ is a substitute for Christ."

Whom did Paul preach, according to 2 Corinthians 4:5?

Why should we be in the business of pointing people to Christ, according to John 10:10?

In our sincere desire to grow in grace, and as we explore the many biblical truths that we need to know in the chapters ahead, we can never forget that we have been called, first and foremost, to a Person.

T H R E E

Abiding in Truth

As we have seen in John 15:4,5, you and I do not have the ability to live the Christian life. Only Christ can. Our role is to surrender to Him. But how does this "surrendering" translate into an objective, intelligent faith that we can get our arms around?

"If you abide in My word, then you are truly disciples of Mine; and you shall know the truth, and the truth shall make you free. . . . If therefore the Son shall make you free, you shall be free indeed" (John 8:31,32,36 NASB).

In what does the above verse tell us to abide?

What will we know?

What will be the result?

Who does it say sets us free?

According to John 1:1, who was in the beginning with God and was God?

In John 1:14, what did the Word become?

If we abide in the Word, according to the above verses in whom are we abiding?

Jesus is the center of the entire written Word of God. He is the living Word. Through the written Word we will find Christ revealing Himself to us. So to abide in His Word is to abide in Him.

Just the Facts

A speaker at a conference I attended exhorted everyone to close their eyes and "think about Jesus." When you think about Jesus, what do you think about? It is important that we do not separate the living Word from the written Word. Christianity is based on facts—truths upon which a person can think or act.

In the following verses, list the facts surrounding the birth and life of Jesus Christ.

Luke 2:2

Luke 2:4

Luke 3:1

Matthew 2:1

Matthew 2:23

Matthew 3:13

Matthew 4:13

Mark 15:22-24

Mark 15:46,47

In the following verses, how did the writer describe himself, and what did he witness?

Acts 2:32

Acts 4:20

1 John 1:1-3

John 21:24

1 Corinthians 15:8

What is the gospel that Paul preached (1 Corinthians 15:1-11)?

If we are not grounded in the objective truth of Scripture, what will we become like, according to Ephesians 4:14?

This is the foundation of our faith. It is rational, intelligent, and open to investigation. If we want to discover the true meaning and experience of "Christ in you," we must learn to take this same objective, clear-thinking faith and bring it into our daily lives.

For us to know the *true* Christ, we must know the *biblical* Christ. Only through the Scriptures can we learn absolute, authoritative truth about God, man, salvation, and life.

A Teachable Spirit and a Spirit Who Teaches

Mere words printed on a page, or the knowledge of doctrines, cannot satisfy the "God-shaped vacuum" in our hearts that cries out for a personal encounter with the living God.

Many people have learned the words of the Bible but have missed Christ. To know Him takes a humble heart.

Why did the Pharisees study the Scriptures, according to John 5:39?

What do the Scriptures testify about?

Why did Jesus say to the Pharisees that if they believed Moses they would believe in Him (John 5:46)?

What did Jesus explain to the two disciples on the way to Emmaus (Luke 24:25-27)?

What did Jesus have to do for the disciples before they could understand the Scriptures (Luke 24:44,45)?

Can we understand the things that come from the Spirit apart from the Spirit of God (1 Corinthians 2:14)?

What does 1 Corinthians 2:9 say about our ability to understand the things God has prepared for those who love Him?

What qualities do we need in order to know Christ better, according to Ephesians 1:17?

Where do we get these qualities?

What attitude must we have to receive the grace of God (James 4:6)?

A true knowledge of Christ and His Word can never come through human intelligence, intellectual ability, or mere study. In fact, we can very easily have a highly trained intellect but still not find Christ.

To grow in grace it is necessary that we realize the Scriptures are God's revelation of truth for our lives. There also needs to be a humble recognition of our dependence upon the Spirit of God, who will enable us to know the God of the Scriptures.

How do we learn about the things God has prepared for us (1 Corinthians 2:10)?

Who knows what a man is thinking (1 Corinthians 2:11)?

In the same way, who knows what God is thinking?

Whom have we received (1 Corinthians 2:12)?

As a result, what can we understand?

What does 1 Corinthians 2:16 say that we also have?

When Christ said that He was going away in John 16:7, whom did He say He would send to us?

What will the Spirit of truth do in our lives (John 16:13)?

What is truth, according to Galatians 2:20?

What is truth, according to Colossians 1:27?

A pastor friend of mine once said that the message of "Christ in you" sounded mystical to him. In reality, there is nothing mystical about Christ in you. It is a fact clearly stated in the Word of God.

Because this is true, we as believers have a new source of power, wisdom, and knowledge in the Person of Christ who lives in us.

FOUR

૭૦૦૭

A New Identity

The issue of identity is inescapable and central to our lives. "Who am I?" we all ask. Identity is often presented under the banner of "self-image." Today the dominant belief is that most people have a "poor self-image," and that the solution is a "good self-image." According to the Bible, what we need is not a *good* self-image, but a *proper* self-image, an identity based on truth.

How does 2 Timothy 3:2 describe people in the last days?

Does this contradict the belief today that what we need is to love ourselves more?

How are we to think about ourselves, according to Romans 12:3?

What does God say that we have become in 2 Corinthians 5:17?

What is the only thing that counts in God's eyes (Galatians 6:15)?

Who Are You?

Only through discovering and resting in our identity as it is taught in the Word of God can we become free from the false identities of this world's system. The Bible teaches us that we have been placed into Christ and are brand-new creatures. But what does that mean to us here and today?

In Christ we have total forgiveness.

What is required for forgiveness to occur, according to Hebrews 9:22?

According to Hebrews 10:12, how many sacrifices for sin did Jesus offer?

Are there any more sacrifices for sin required (Hebrews 10:18).

What do we have, therefore, in Christ (Ephesians 1:7; Colossians 1:14)?

In Christ we have been given His righteousness.

What did God make Christ to be for us (2 Corinthians 5:21)?

What do we become in Christ?

As a result of Christ's death, what have we been made (Romans 5:19)?

Those who are baptized into Christ are clothed with what, according to Galatians 3:27?

When God looks at us, what does He see?

What does Hebrews 10:14 say we have been made by the sacrifice of Christ?

In Christ we have forgiveness and the righteousness of Christ. How acceptable, then, are we to God?

In Christ we have become children of God.

What right is given to those who believe and receive Jesus (John 1:12,13)?

How does it say children of God are born?

What spirit did we receive, according to Romans 8:15,16?

By Him we cry what?

What does the Spirit of God testify to our spirits that we are?

What then is our identity? Who are we?

In Christ we have total access to the throne of grace.

Because we are in Christ, how can we approach God (Ephesians 3:12)?

How should we approach the throne of grace, according to Hebrews 4:16?

What will we find there?

From where does our confidence to enter the Most Holy Place come, according to Hebrews 10:19?

We are made alive together with Christ.

How does the Bible describe you and me before we came to know Christ (Ephesians 2:1)?

What does a dead man need?

What does 1 Corinthians 15:22 say happens to those in Christ?

Because of God's great love for us, what did He make us, even though we were dead in our transgressions (Ephesians 2:4,5)?

What is the wages of sin (Romans 6:23)?

What is the gift of God?

In Christ you have a brand-new identity. You are a child of God, totally forgiven, clothed in the righteousness of Christ, fully alive, with total access to the throne of grace. This is a proper self-image, a foundation based on truth. These truths are foundational for growing in grace.

What is our identity, according to Ephesians 5:8?

How should we then live?

What are we to put on (Ephesians 4:24)?

As God's chosen people, holy and dearly loved, what are we to clothe ourselves with (Colossians 3:12-14)?

As dearly loved children, what kind of life are we to live (Ephesians 5:1,2)?

A knowledge of the believer's identity in Christ is an essential foundation block of the Christian life. J.E. lived for years in fear, anger, and bitterness. But he experienced a dramatic turn-around when his eyes were opened to the wonderful identity that was his as a child of God. Before he died, J.E. was able to reach out to his family and see God make peace by healing the years of hurt, anger, and resentment. In his life we can see that the gospel is truly "the power of God for the salvation of everyone who believes" (Romans 1:16).

F I V E

Faith Illustrated

There are striking parallels between an unborn baby's dependence on its mother and our life of dependence while growing in grace.

Where is our life to be found, according to John 1:4?

What is the testimony God has given in 1 John 5:11,12?

Where is this eternal life found?

How does the Bible describe our relationship with the world in John 17:15,16?

What will happen to the world and its desires, according to 1 John 2:17?

The world is filled with tribulation. But according to John 16:33, who has overcome the world?

What reason does 1 John 4:4 give that we have overcome the world?

What should our attitude be toward our lives in this world (Philippians 1:21)?

Because of its dependent life, a baby in the womb could say, "For me to live is Mom." In the same way, because of our life-line—the Holy Spirit—we can say with the apostle Paul, "For me to live is Christ."

The New Testament consistently tells us first who we are, then exhorts us to present ourselves to God in dependent faith. Learning to walk in these truths does not happen overnight; it requires the ongoing ministry of the Holy Spirit through the Scriptures.

Galatians 2:20 tells us that our part in living out our faith is to "live by faith in the Son of God." There are three qualities that will help us get a handle on this: dependency, objectivity, and availability.

The Life of a Perfect Man

Like the baby in the womb of its mother, and like the branch that is abiding in the vine, our life in Christ is a totally dependent life. Jesus Christ showed us how to live a dependent life. Although He was and is God, when He lived here on this earth He lived as a perfect man, in total dependence upon His Father.

In John 1:1, who was in the beginning?

Who was the Word with?

In John 1:14, what happened to the Word?

From the context of this passage, who do you believe the Word was?

Even though Jesus is God, according to John 5:30, how much did He say He could do on His own?

According to John 5:19, how much can the Son do by Himself?

What is the only thing He can do?

How did Christ live while He was here on the earth?

In John 16:7, why did Jesus say it was good that He was going away?

And in Galatians 2:20, who is it that now lives in us?

How are we to live, according to John 15:5?

What will be the result in our lives?

What is the fruit of the Spirit of God in Galatians 5:22,23?

How much fruit can a person bear apart from Christ?

Read the description of God's kind of love in 1 Corinthians 13:4-8. Now, before each description of love, insert the words "I am."

How much of this type of love can we produce on our own?

Apart from Christ we can do nothing. If you have any doubts about a life of total dependence, I cannot recommend any greater proof than simply trying to love people with God's kind of love.

Swallowing and Faith

Someone could say, "Swallowing makes you live," and that sounds right. Swallowing food does enable me to live. However, I could also swallow poison and die. So it isn't the swallowing itself that nourishes me; it is the *object* of my swallowing—food—that gives strength to my body.

Faith is like swallowing. It is not my faith itself but the *object* of my faith that saves me.

In whom does John 3:16 say we must believe in order to have eternal life?

In John 5:24, what do we have to hear and in whom do we have to believe to have eternal life?

Where is the power of God contained, according to Romans 1:16?

When Paul came to the Corinthians, what attitude did he come with (1 Corinthians 2:3)?

What was his message a demonstration of (1 Corinthians 2:4)?

Where then does our faith rest (1 Corinthians 2:5)?

How are we born again, according to 1 Peter 1:23?

What does Peter say about the Word of God in 1 Peter 1:25?

According to the above verses, what is the object of our faith?

What does Matthew 17:20 tell us about how important the size of a person's faith is?

The issue is not how much faith we have. In fact, to emphasize the amount of a person's faith is an insult to God. Rather, the issue is *the greatness of the God in whom we believe*. The issue is the *object* of our faith. The object of the Christian's faith is the Lord Jesus Christ and His Word.

A Life of Availability

One of our conferences was attended by a blind woman named Marda and her Seeing Eye dog, Zesty. Each day Marda would sit at her table and Zesty would lie at her feet for hours— sometimes sleeping, sometimes looking around, but never leaving her post. Whenever we stopped for a break or a meal, however, Zesty was instantly alert and on the job. All Marda had to say was "Zesty," and off they went.

That faithful dog has been a terrific example to me of the way I want to be responsive and available to the Lord. This is our role.

What was the question the disciples came and asked Jesus in John 6:28?

How did Jesus answer in verse 29?

What did God say about Jesus at His baptism in Mark 1:11?

At this point in Jesus' life, had He healed anyone, performed any miracles, or preached any sermons?

Do you think He was available to do so if His Father wanted Him to?

What does Romans 12:1 say is our reasonable act of worship?

What does 1 Peter 3:15 say we are to do in our hearts?

What should we always be prepared or available to do?

Do we know when we will be called upon to give an account of the hope that is in us?

What, therefore, is our role?

What does Hebrews 11:6 say it takes to please God?

Again, as children of God, what is our role?

Dependency, objectivity, and availability. These are the characteristics of our faith. The decision to present ourselves to Him by faith is our part in the process of growing in grace. God produces the results.

SIX

~∞~

Feelings in Focus

Sometimes we hear people say, "Don't confuse me with the facts! My mind is already made up." We are all capable of falling into this way of thinking, and we can correct it only by a sincere commitment to truth.

Seeing Is Not Believing

In the story of Jesus raising Lazarus from the dead, recorded in John 11:47,48, what did the Pharisees say upon hearing the news?

Did the Pharisees deny that Jesus performed a miracle? So was the Pharisees' problem a lack of evidence?

269

What did they fear would happen if they let Jesus continue His ministry?

How does Jesus describe Himself in John 14:6?

Were the Pharisees more interested in truth or in their job security?

In Luke 16:30, what did the rich man say would convince his brothers to repent?

What was Abraham's response in Luke 16:31?

Those Crazy Emotions

Emotions are the most vivid aspect of our experience. When we are in the middle of intense feelings, they seem like ultimate reality—so much so that when feelings and facts don't agree, feelings usually get the deciding vote. This being true, it is important for us to know how our emotions operate.

The last time you were at a scary movie, did what you see and hear on the screen actually happen?

How did you feel, though?

What were your emotions responding to?

Would you have felt scared or frightened if you had not seen the images on the screen?

So are your emotions initiators or responders?

What does Jesus tell us not to worry about in Matthew 6:34?

When we worry about tomorrow, how do we feel today?

What did Paul say we should do about the past in Philippians 3:13?

How does thinking about the past control how we feel today?

Can our emotions discern the past, the present, or the future?

What does Paul say is sufficient for us in 2 Corinthians 12:9?

When is this grace sufficient—in the past, present, or future?

So where do our minds need to be in order to draw on the sufficiency of God's grace?

Emotions are responders. They only *respond* to what we put into our minds. They can't discern the difference between fact and fantasy or past, present, and future. Knowing this helps us see how important it is to protect our minds.

My dad taught me this lesson once when he abruptly closed the book he was reading. I asked him why. He responded by asking me if I would eat garbage. Then he said, "Neither will I eat garbage with my mind."

We need to protect our minds so that we can live according to truth rather than our feelings.

A New Order

Contrary to the order of events in our subjective thinking, the Word of God exhorts us to live in the opposite order. Rather than waiting around to "get excited" or to "feel like it," *we are to step out by faith in obedience to God's Word.* Then, finally, we will find our feelings responding to that step of faith.

There are very few things in the Word of God that we can honestly say we feel like doing when we first encounter them. For instance:

How does Matthew 5:44 say we should respond to our enemies?

What do our emotions normally lead us to want to do to our enemies?

What does Matthew 20:26,27 say about those who want to become great and be first among you?

What do we normally tend to do instead?

What does Romans 12:20 say to do if your enemy is hungry or thirsty?

Caught up in the emotions of controversy, what do we normally want to do to our enemies instead of feeding them and quenching their thirst?

To whom does Romans 13:1,7 say everyone must submit himself?

Who is it that has established all authority?

How do we usually *feel* like responding to authority . . . especially at tax time each year?

What does James 1:22 say we should do with the Word of God?

What is God's promise to those who put His Word into practice (James 1:25)?

How does Jesus describe someone who puts His Word into practice (Matthew 7:24)?

In Hebrews 5:12, what did the writer say about the maturity level of the Hebrew converts?

Who does Hebrews 5:14 say solid food is for?

How have the mature trained themselves to distinguish good from evil?

Growth in grace comes to those who, through a totally dependent faith in Christ, put the truth of God into practice. It is the exact opposite of the world's philosophy: "If it feels good, do it." Learning to live objectively—keeping our *feelings* in focus, presenting our minds to be renewed by the truth of God's Word, and then stepping out by faith—is at the heart of *growing in grace.*

SEVEN

✧✦✧

Conflict Within

Regardless of all that Christ has done and taught us, *we still have sin within us;* we *never* grow to a point where we are incapable of sinning in this earthly life. As we grow in grace we actually become more aware of the evil within us.

Read Romans 7:15-24.

What trap did Paul find himself in, according to verse 15?

What caused him to do the things he did not want to do (verse 17)?

As a result, what did he conclude about his flesh (verse 18)?

What law or principle did he find at work within him (verse 21)?

What conclusion did he come to about himself (verse 24)?

In concluding "wretched man that I am," what question was Paul forced to ask?

From his question, did Paul think he had the ability to rescue himself?

In 1 Timothy 1:15, how did Paul describe himself?

Who did he say came into this world to save sinners?

Who then can rescue us from the trap of "the things I want to do I do not do, and the things I hate I do"?

What was Paul's conclusion in Romans 7:25?

Does God show us the truth about ourselves to condemn us (Romans 8:1)?

God allows us to see more and more into our hearts and to discover the truth that apart from Him we really can do nothing. But none of this is meant to drive us to despair or to condemn us. God shows us the truth about ourselves so that we will learn to live dependently upon Christ for the life that only He can live.

Conflict Within

We can all identify with Paul's struggle expressed in Romans 7. But the questions still remain: Why do I still sin? Why do I still have temptations?

If someone is in Christ, what does the Bible say he has become (2 Corinthians 5:17)?

According to John 3:5-8, when we are born again, what are we born of?

If Christ is in you, what part of you is made alive (Romans 8:10)?

What does this verse say about our bodies?

According to the above verses, what part of us is made new?

What does this tell you about your soul and body? Are they born again or made new?

What does Paul say lives in this flesh of ours (Romans 7:20)?

If sin lives in us, can we then think, feel, and do the same old things we did as a lost person?

As a result of sin living in us, describe the struggle we have as Christians (Galatians 5:17).

How does Peter describe this same conflict in 1 Peter 2:11?

When we know the nature of the flesh, should it surprise us when we sin or are tempted to sin?

The truth regarding indwelling sin is rather strong medicine, but it helps us learn that we can never live the Christian life on our own. You and I will not be free from the influence of sin until the Lord Jesus gives us new bodies. Until then, we can grow in grace.

AM or FM?

When you come face-to-face with indwelling sin, you see the importance of the truth I shared in the first chapter: *You grow in grace as you focus on what God is doing in the midst of what you are doing.* The answer is not in ourselves; the answer is found in looking to our Savior and Lord, Jesus Christ.

In Galatians 5:16, how does Paul encourage us to walk as children of God?

When we walk by the Spirit, what does it say we will not do?

Does it say your desires will go away?

In Matthew 15:19, Jesus lists several manifestations of the fruit of the flesh. Where did He say these things originate?

If these things originate in the heart, how much sense does it make to try to clean up the flesh (the external)?

How did the Galatians try to clean up the flesh (Galatians 3:3).

What did Paul call them?

When you are trying to clean up the flesh, where is the focus of your mind?

In Romans 6:11-13, how are we to consider ourselves in relation to sin?

How are we to consider ourselves in relation to Christ?

Since we are alive to Christ, do we have to obey sin's evil desires?

Describe the choice we have as children of God in Romans 6:13.

In Romans 6:14, Paul offers encouragement with the reminder that "sin shall not be your master." Why is that true, according to this passage?

As children of God, we have a choice. When we walk in the Spirit, offering ourselves to God, we cannot at the same time fulfill the desires of the flesh.

It's much like an AM/FM radio. I can't determine the programming, but I can choose which one I will tune in.

A Warning

The Bible teaches that we are engaged in spiritual warfare. The conflict within is deeper than a battle against our own sinful desire. It is a battle of truth versus error, and the battleground is the minds of people.

In John 8:31,32, what will we know if we hold to Christ's teaching?

What will the truth do?

If truth sets you free, what binds you?

How does 1 Peter 5:8 describe Satan?

How does Jesus describe Satan in John 8:44?

Is there any truth in Satan?

According to 2 Corinthians 11:3, what tactic did Satan use on Eve?

Therefore, what is the only way Satan can devour us?

How are we to worship God, according to John 4:24?

If we are going to "walk by the Spirit," what will we be walking in?

Based on these verses, do you see the importance of "walking in truth"?

With the nature of our flesh, what attitude should we have toward others caught in a sin (Galatians 6:1)?

This whole discussion of indwelling sin is a necessary building block of growing in grace. We absolutely must come face-to-face with our own inability before we will ever turn to Christ for His ability! That's why there is no greater sign that a person is genuinely growing in grace than when with humble tears he discovers the reality that he is a "wretched man." The only people who truly know this are those who are coming to know the Lord Jesus in an intimate way.

EIGHT

❦

Sustained by Hope

Another important biblical building block for growing in grace is hope. It is something the world does not have and cannot give.

But what is hope? What does it mean, and how does it relate to growing in grace?

The Meaning of Hope

It is hope that gives us God's perspective on life. Part of the confusion over the meaning of hope arises out of the watered-down definition used in everyday speech. "I *hope* I get a promotion at work." "I *hope* I get a puppy for Christmas." "I *hope* it doesn't rain today."

How does Paul define our blessed hope in Titus 2:13?

What does Romans 8:23-25 say that we wait eagerly for?

Is this hope based on what we see or on what we already have?

What is our hope concerning those who have fallen asleep (1 Thessalonians 4:13,14)?

What is the hope of those who are alive at the coming of the Lord (1 Thessalonians 4:17,18)?

Why did John write "Do not let your hearts be troubled" in John 14:1-4?

Before Jesus went to prepare a place for us, what else were we assured of (John 14:3)?

What will we be like when Christ appears, according to 1 John 3:2?

How does this hope cause us to live here and today (1 John 3:3)?

In the Bible, hope is man's eager expectation that something which God has promised will certainly happen in the future. There is never any "maybe" or "hope so" about it. True hope is where God said, "This will be," and we live in excited anticipation until it comes to pass.

Who Does the Holding?

Several years ago at Yosemite National Park, my son, Bobby, asked me to take him rock-climbing. Bobby was only six at the time, and I would never have trusted him to hold on to me. He didn't have the strength or the balance. I intended to hold on to him.

In the same way, our salvation rests on Jesus Christ's faithfulness to hold on to us.

How does Peter describe the hope that we have as a result of our new birth (1 Peter 1:3-5)?

Why does Peter call it a living hope?

As a result of our new birth, what kind of inheritance do we have?

Whose power keeps this inheritance for us?

For those in Christ, what did God do to guarantee our inheritance (Ephesians 1:13,14)?

In Philippians 1:6, who has promised to complete the work in us?

How does Paul describe the One who has called us in 1 Thessalonians 5:24?

In 1 Corinthians 1:8, who will keep us strong to the end, blameless on the day of our Lord Jesus Christ?

Can He be depended on to keep us strong (1 Corinthians 1:9)?

Hope for Today

Kay was a beautiful girl in her mid-twenties who came to me for counseling about her alcohol problem. We discussed her understanding of salvation, and finally I said, "Kay, your problem is not one of behavior; your problem is one of identity."

The first area of our lives where God wants to build into us a secure hope is in our assurance of salvation. When Kay understood the difference between her behavior and her identity, hope became a reality for her. Once you understand your identity, you can face the daily trials and struggles of the Christian life with confidence.

What is our hope of glory, according to Colossians 1:27?

When we are going through trials today, who is there with us?

Is Christ bigger than the trials we are facing (1 John 4:4)?

What is this hope called in Hebrews 6:19?

Since we have been justified through faith, what relationship do we have with God through Jesus Christ (Romans 5:1-5)?

In what do we now stand?

What is the hope that we rejoice in?

As a result, what should be our response to suffering?

What are the attributes that suffering produces?

Why does Romans 5:5 say that hope does not disappoint us?

According to Romans 8:29,30, to what role did God predestine those He foreknew?

According to Romans 5:1-5 and James 1:2-4, does the process of conforming us into the likeness of His Son occur during times of suffering?

Some people might say that this hope gives us a license to sin. But we are more than forgiven sinners. We have been made new, just like the caterpillar that has been made into a butterfly. We have Christ living in us, and He is our hope of glory.

In Hebrews 8:10, what did God promise to do with His law?

According to 2 Peter 1:4, what have Christians become partakers of or participants in?

In 1 Corinthians 6:17, what did Paul say about the one who unites himself with the Lord?

What does 2 Corinthians 5:17 say about anyone who is in Christ?

For the true child of God, the message of our secure hope in Christ is fuel for his inner fire and food for his deepest hunger—to be everything that God wants him to be. Only with a secure hope, rooted in the faithfulness of God, will we be able to weather the storms of life.

The Christian life is *empowered* by Christ and *fueled* by faith— our attitude of total dependence upon the indwelling Christ to live out His life in and through us. However, it is our total confidence that Christ will *complete* the work He began in us which enables us to persevere over a lifetime. Without hope, people give up. But for the person who is growing in grace, the Christian life is always *sustained* by hope.

NINE

*Freedom
from Guilt*

We Christians absolutely must come to an understanding of God's forgiveness and acceptance in Christ before we can go on to grow in grace.

I like to state it this way: *Until you rest in the finality of the cross, you will never experience the reality of the resurrection, which is Christ Himself living in and through you.* Unless you rest in the fact that Jesus did it all, you will be so busy trying to "pay off your debt" (atone for your sins) that you will never grow in and enjoy the personal relationship that Christ has provided for you. Let us explore why this is so and examine some of the truths in which we must abide in order to continue growing in grace. The necessary background for these truths is an understanding of the Old and New Covenants.

Only a Shadow

Read Hebrews 10:5-8.

Who is speaking, according to verse 5?

Did God desire sacrifices and sin offerings, according to verse 8?

Were they pleasing to God?

Did the law require sacrifices to be made, according to verse 8?

Why were the sacrifices necessary, according to Hebrews 9:22?

What were the sacrifices a reminder of, according to Hebrews 10:3?

According to Hebrews 9:13, were the animal sacrifices able to sanctify (set apart) the worshipers outwardly or inwardly?

Were the sacrifices offered under the Old Covenant to apply for a designated period of time, according to Hebrews 9:10?

If so, how long were they to apply (verse 10)?

According to Hebrews 10:4,11, could the sacrifices offered again and again take away sin?

Were the animal sacrifices able to clear the conscience of the worshiper, according to Hebrews 9:9?

Read Hebrews 10:1,2.

Did the sacrifices offered under the Old Covenant make the worshiper perfect in God's sight (verse 1)?

If they could have made the worshiper perfect, would there have been a need to continue offering them (verse 2)?

According to the same verse, if the worshiper had been made perfect by the animal sacrifices, would he have felt guilty for his sins?

In Stewart's situation, what was the emotional result of having an unpaid debt for the wrong he committed?

As in Stewart's example, when we are constantly reminded of our failures by someone, is it possible to develop a positive relationship with him or her?

Like Stewart's dollar-a-week payments, the Old Testament worshipers had to make continual offerings for their guilt. But even though these sacrifices brought a certain amount of relief from fear of punishment, they were at the same time an "annual reminder of sins." The Day of Atonement for the Israelite was not a day of rejoicing; it was a day of concentration on failures, of confession and mourning over sins. It was a day of regret. Like Stewart, who could not pay his future dollar-a-week payments as a lump sum, the Israelite could not bring a sacrifice for his future failures. The best he could hope for was to be clean up-to-date.

Better in Every Way!

If you were to read straight through the New Testament book of Hebrews, one word would continue to jump out at you: *better*. Though the Old Covenant, also called the law of Moses, was clearly given by God, it was a temporary system to prepare Israel for the coming of the Messiah, who would bring in a new relationship between God and man that would be far superior. In Hebrews, Jesus Christ, the Son of God, is presented not only as being better in His Person, but in His priesthood as well. He brought in a better covenant; He offered a better sacrifice; and all His works have been "founded on better promises" (Hebrews 8:6). The Person and work of Jesus Christ are better in every way! One of the most dramatic contrasts between the two covenants can be seen in the issue of forgiveness.

According to Hebrews 9:15, who is the mediator of the New Covenant?

When did the New Covenant go into effect (Hebrews 9:16,17)?

How does Hebrews 10:20 describe this new agreement between God and man?

How did God intend to do away with sin, according to Hebrews 9:26?

According to this same verse, how many times did Christ appear in order to deal with sins?

What period of time did Jesus' final sacrifice for sin cover, according to Hebrews 10:12?

What was Jesus' sacrifice able to accomplish that the Old Covenant could not?

Hebrews 9:14:

Hebrews 10:14:

How does John 1:29 describe Jesus?

According to 1 John 3:5, why did Jesus come?

According to Hebrews 10:18, is there any further sacrifice necessary for our sins?

Under the New Covenant, what does God say He will no longer remember (Hebrews 10:17)?

According to Hebrews 9:14, what is the result in our lives of having our conscience cleansed (being free from guilt)?

What do you conclude about the sin issue between you and God?

Like Stewart, do you still feel there is an unpaid debt between you and God?

Is your understanding of forgiveness more like atonement, which covered sins, or the completed work on the cross, which did away with them?

Christ has done for us what could never have been accomplished under the law. He has accomplished total and final forgiveness of sins for us, not just for the past, but for our entire lives, including past, present, and future sins.

The Bible from beginning to end describes a God who loves mankind, who is longsuffering, patient, and merciful in His dealings with our rebellious race. However, the same Scriptures also depict a God who is perfectly holy and absolutely just, who "does not leave the guilty unpunished" (Exodus 34:7). How can He do both? Granted that He loves man and wants to save him, how can He do so without compromising His holiness or relaxing His standards—in short, without denying Himself? The answer lies in "propitiation."

"Propitiation" is an unfamiliar word to most people; however, it is vitally important in understanding the gospel and God's attitude toward you. The central meaning of the word is "satisfaction."

The Big Picture

According to 1 Peter 3:18, for whom did Christ die?

Read Isaiah 53:3-6.

According to this passage, who took the full wrath of God for our sins?

What was the benefit granted to us by Jesus taking the punishment for our sins (verse 5)?

According to 1 John 2:2, who is the propitiation (atoning sacrifice for all of our sins)?

What did God demonstrate to us through the cross, according to Romans 5:8?

According to Romans 3:25, what did God also demonstrate to us through the cross?

According to Romans 3:26, whom did God choose to be the justifier or the One who declares us righteous?

In regard to this same verse, does God see His choice of Jesus as the "justifier" as a just or fair way of dealing with our sins?

As far as God is concerned, can you conclude that God's justice was honored through the cross?

If God is fully satisfied, are you?

Imagine a judge in his robe, gavel in hand, as he presides over cases all day in a local court. He calls for the next case and there stands his own son, accused of a serious traffic offense. What is the judge's role? He must determine whether the defendant is guilty or innocent, and if guilty, see that justice is carried out. In this case the evidence is conclusive. "Guilty as charged," says the judge. The case is closed and punishment is declared. The judge has done his job. But then an unusual thing happens. The judge stands, removes his robe, and walks around to the front of the court. He pulls out his checkbook and writes a check to pay his son's fine. As a judge, he made sure that justice was honored; as a father, he paid his son's debt. Here you see a tremendous picture of how God could forgive sinners without compromising His perfect justice: The cross was God's answer to both.

The Result in Our Lives

To teach that Jesus did it all is not to be "light on sin." It is to say that God poured out every ounce of His holy hatred and wrath toward people's sins upon His Son, who was bearing our judgment for us. Now, because Christ did pay it all, God can say that He is fully satisfied, and can deal with us without judging us for our sins: "Since we have now been justified by His blood, how much more shall we be saved from God's wrath through Him!" (Romans 5:9).

Get a Move On

Read 1 John 4:18.

Where is there no fear?

What does perfect love drive out?

Why does perfect love drive out fear?

What will be the result to the individual who fears?

Do you think that you will draw near to God if you are fearing His wrath or punishment?

Once again, look at Hebrews 9:14. What was the result of having our consciences cleansed (being free from guilt) through the sacrifice of Christ?

As we grow in grace and in the knowledge of what Jesus Christ has done for us, it becomes increasingly clear that the most natural and reasonable thing to do is to give ourselves without reserve to our Lord for His use. But we absolutely must rest by faith in the complete acceptance of what Jesus has purchased for us if we are going to continue growing in grace. Unless we rest in the finality of the cross, we will never experience the reality of the resurrection—Christ living His life through us!

TEN
ʊʊ

Freedom and Maturity

For almost 2000 years the church has been plagued by the pressure to return to Galatianism. (Galatianism is, after having come to salvation by faith, returning to the law in an effort to perfect yourself.) The greatest practical problem you face in persuading people to abandon Galatianism is that being under the law produces an *appearance* of maturity and character in them.

Is the Law Good?

What question did Paul ask concerning the law in Romans 7:7?

How did Paul answer this question (verses 7,12)?

Was the law made for the lost or the saved (verse 9)?

Read Romans 3:19,20.

To whom does the law speak, according to verse 19?

Can anyone be declared righteous in God's sight by observing the law (verse 28)?

What is the function of the law, according to verse 20?

According to Galatians 3:24, what was the purpose of the law?

Once the law has shown us we are sinners and then brought us to Christ, has it done its work?

According to Galatians 3:25, once the law has done its work, are we under its supervision any longer?

Dying to the Law

According to 1 Corinthians 15:56, what is the power of sin?

Is the law sin (Romans 7:7,8)?

Can the law change a person's heart?

What does trying to keep the law produce within us (verse 8)?

In Romans 7:5, what arouses the sinful passions at work in our bodies?

Read Colossians 2:20-23.

Can adherence to laws make a person look good on the outside?

Do they have value in restraining sensual indulgences?

We have seen that the law is not bad. Paul says in 1 Timothy 1:8, "We know that the law is good if one uses it properly." It is misused when it is used to produce an outward conformity in the absence of faith, hope, and love.

According to Galatians 2:19, what have we as Christians died to?

What is the purpose for dying to the law?

Something Better Has Come!

It is important that we emphasize what God has *added* above and beyond the removal of the law. God's method of releasing us from the law is to replace it with His indwelling life.

Read Galatians 4:1-7.

What analogy did Paul use to show the relationship of the law to believers?

What are we now called, having been redeemed from the law (verse 5)?

Since we have full rights as sons, are we subject to the basic principles of the world?

Whom has God placed in our hearts so that we may call God "Abba, Father" (verse 6)?

Read 2 Corinthians 3:6-11.

According to verse 7, did the law come with glory?

How is the glory of the New Covenant described, according to verses 9 and 10?

Read Galatians 5:16-18.

How are we to live, according to verse 16?

According to verse 18, if you are led by the Spirit, what are you not under?

Is God's answer to our every need or circumstance a principle or a Person?

Rather than trying to live by laws or principles, how are we to live, according to Galatians 2:20,21?

Falling Flat on My Face

Going through trials is how we grow! Yes, if you teach the freedom that is ours in Christ, a certain number of immature people will try to take advantage of it for a while. But by falling flat on their faces, they will learn how stupid sin really is. However, if we are teaching people how to walk according to the indwelling life of Christ, those who try to take advantage will be the exception, not the rule.

According to Romans 5:3,4, what is it that develops character in our lives?

Read James 1:2-4.

How are we to view difficult times (verse 2)?

What does the testing of our faith develop (verse 3)?

When you persevere in truth (hold on to truth), what is the end result (verse 4)?

According to John 6:29, what is the work of God?

During trials, do you at times feel it is "work" to believe God (trust in Him, rely upon Him)?

Have difficulties in your life caused you to see your own inadequacies?

According to Hebrews 13:20,21, what will God equip us with?

According to Romans 8:38,39, can anything we do or not do separate us from God's love?

According to Romans 8:28, will God work some things or all things for our good?

Who does Hebrews 13:5 say will never leave us or forsake us?

When do you think we learn the extent of God's love and acceptance—through our successes or through our failures?

When you have fallen flat on your face and are able to see that God still loves and accepts you—that He still believes the best about you (1 Corinthians 13:7)—do you think this will cause you to be drawn more to Him and to trust Him more in your life?

According to John 3:30, who must become greater?

God cares about you. There is nothing you can give Him, there is no service you can perform, there is no self-discipline you can apply that He wants more than He wants *you.* He wants to reveal Himself and His love to you, and He wants you to grow to love Him in return. That is how we grow in grace.

ELEVEN

৩৯৫৬

Food for Growth

Many Christians make themselves absolute emotional wrecks worrying over the progress they think they should be making in their Christian growth. But you cannot *make* yourself grow spiritually any more than you can make yourself grow physically.

It's God's Business

It is important to remember that we do not grow ourselves.

Read Romans 8:28,29.

How often is God working for our good?

According to these verses, in what situations will God not be working for our good?

In verse 29, what does Paul say is God's plan for those who know Him?

Therefore, whose responsibility is it to conform us to "the image of His Son"?

What is Paul confident of, according to Philippians 1:6?

Who began "the work" in us?

How long will He continue to carry it out?

When will completion occur?

Therefore, who is responsible for your spiritual growth?

My Response to God's Ability

This is not to say that we have *no* decision to make or role to play. In Philippians 2:12, what does Paul urge the saints in Philippi to do?

What should be their motivation, according to Philippians 2:13?

Who is the initiator of the Christian life?

What is man's role?

A good way to paraphrase these verses is: "In a humble and dependent attitude, work out on the outside of your life what God is doing on the inside." We do not grow ourselves. God is inside us "to will and to do according to His good purpose." Our role is to walk in an intimate, loving, faith relationship with our heavenly Father, and to cooperate with what He is doing in our lives.

In our spiritual lives, we cannot make ourselves grow in grace either, but we can do certain things: We can eat good food, exercise, and enjoy walking through life as a child of God as He grows us in His time. But what do I mean by "eating good food"?

Getting to Know Christ

In all my years in school, I never studied my biology textbook to learn about the author. I studied to learn enough biology to pass the exam; I didn't know or care about the scientist who wrote it. However, the Bible is strikingly different. The purpose of studying God's Word is, first and foremost, to get to know the Author.

In John 17:3, what did Jesus say was eternal life?

According to 1 John 5:20, why did Jesus come to give us understanding of His truth?

In Philippians 3:8, what does Paul consider as having the greatest importance?

How does he view everything else in comparison?

What does Paul pray for in Ephesians 1:17?

What do these verses indicate should be the goal of our Bible study?

Don't fall for the deception of believing that we start out with Christ, then "graduate" to the "deep things" of God. *Jesus Christ is everything.* There's nothing "deeper" than knowing Him intimately! That's what we will do throughout eternity—discover and enjoy the wonders of Him. We'll never get to the end of all that He is.

Majoring on the Majors

It sounds strange, but not all of the tangents which cause Christians to stray away from Christ are unbiblical. We can actually get off on *biblical* truth. It is absolutely imperative that we teach *biblical truths according to the proper emphases given to them in the Scriptures.* So what are the "majors" in the Word of God?

In John 13:34,35, what was Jesus' priority?

What did Jesus say would be the way His disciples could be identified?

How are we to love?

According to John 15:9, how does Christ love us?

How do you think the Father has loved Christ?

How then would you conclude we are to love others (John 15:12,13)?

How did Paul describe the extent of God's love for us in Romans 8:35-39?

In 1 John 4:9, how did God show His love to us?

How is this love a motivation for us to love each other (1 John 4:11,19)?

In 1 Corinthians 13:1-3, Paul writes of several things that people would consider important. Yet how important are these without love?

Why should love be the highest priority of a Christian, according to 1 Corinthians 13:13?

How did John summarize the commandments of God in 1 John 3:23?

Since the Bible gives great emphasis to teaching the Person and work of Jesus Christ, and loving one another as He loved us, those are the things we should emphasize. If we will give ourselves to study and concentration on God's greatest directives, we will find that He teaches us the lesser issues as well, and our understanding will be balanced according to the biblical pattern.

TWELVE

ᘐᕽᕽᘗ

Abundant Life Today

I once received a short note from someone in Nigeria. In halting and misspelled English it said:

> Deer Bob George. That is the most sweetums name under heven. Angles and sky rejois at yor most Christan life. Will you send me a watch?

Too many of us approach prayer much like this letter. We use flattery or follow some formula in order to get what we want from God. But what is true biblical prayer?

Read Matthew 6:5-8.

For what purpose do the hypocrites in verse 5 pray?

In contrast, how are we to pray (verse 6)?

What is the result of praying to your Father in secret?

For what purpose do the pagans babble when they pray, according to verse 7?

What is the reason we do not have to be like the pagans when we pray (verse 8)?

According to these verses, what do you conclude is our basis for prayer?

What attitude does the parable of the Pharisee and tax collector in Luke 18:9-14 teach us we should pray with?

In John 14:13,14, whose name are we to pray in?

What is the promise in these verses for those who pray in Jesus' name?

What reason does James give that we do not receive our requests when we ask (James 4:3)?

In whose name is this type of prayer prayed?

Why do you think Scripture says to pray in Jesus' name?

What is the confidence we have as children of God in approaching God in prayer, according to 1 John 5:14,15?

This confidence comes through praying according to whose will?

What did Jesus ask of His Father in Matthew 26:39?

Whose will was Christ most interested in seeing carried out?

Which verse, James 4:3 or Matthew 26:39, best describes the attitude in which you approach God in prayer?

According to John 15:7, where should our requests to God come from?

Where are we going to learn what the will of God is?

Who then is the initiator of true biblical prayer?

How often are we to pray, according to 1 Thessalonians 5:17?

From the above study, what do you conclude about biblical prayer?

My dad taught me all he knew about conservative politics. We discussed political philosophies for hours. What my father taught me I talked back to him. The enjoyment that we shared in those discussions was from the meeting of our minds as we talked. And I have come to see prayer in much the same light.

Prayer is inspired by God speaking to us through His written Word. Then we pray God's Word back to Him as it relates to our own personal lives, heartaches, needs, and aspirations. We pray in a humble attitude, trusting the Lord to teach us and answer us according to His will.

Remember, there are no rigid rules to prayer. God loves you. Talk to Him. Pray continually. Ask anything according to His will. As you do, watch your confidence grow in the reliability of His Word and your appreciation for His gentleness, faithfulness, mercy, kindness, and love.

What's Spiritual?

According to the common mindset there is a division between "spiritual" and "secular." Spiritual activities are things such as going to church, reading your Bible, praying, and giving. Most other activities, such as work and family activities, count as secular.

Spirituality, however, is not determined by the *type* of activity but by the *source* of the activity. Christ lives in you. You can enjoy your relationship with the Lord wherever you are.

In John 4:19,20, where did the Samaritan woman say her ancestors and the Jews worshiped?

In contrast, how did Jesus say that the true worshipers would worship the Father (John 4:23)?

What is the reason that we must worship God in spirit and in truth (John 4:24)?

Where can this take place?

List the places where you regularly go during the week. Can you worship God in spirit and truth in these places?

In 2 Thessalonians 3:10, what does God say a man must do?

What is the directive given in Ephesians 4:28?

What is the purpose of work, according to this verse?

Who tells us to go to work?

What can we then conclude about work? Is it a spiritual or a secular activity?

What does 1 Corinthians 3:16 say that we have become?

Who lives in us?

How does Paul describe our bodies in 1 Corinthians 6:19,20?

Who lives in us?

What does Romans 12:5 say that we who are many have become?

How did we get to be a part of the body of Christ, according to 1 Corinthians 12:13?

As the body of Christ, what does Ephesians 4:4-6 say that we share in common?

What is our fellowship based on when we gather on Sunday?

Where is the church—born-again believers—on Monday morning?

Where is Christ when His body is gathered together on Sunday morning?

Where is Christ on Monday morning?

What can you conclude about this so-called division between secular and spiritual?

The Christian life is Christ. It is knowing Him and walking in Him in a relationship which touches every aspect of life in the world. If we will give ourselves to Him in an attitude of dependence, we will discover the exciting experience of watching Him use us in our everyday lives. All day every day is an opportunity to grow in grace and in the knowledge of our Lord Jesus Christ.

THIRTEEN

∽∾

Marks of Growth

Only those who have first received the love and grace of God can go on to become willing servants and "ministers of reconciliation" (2 Corinthians 5:18) even to bitter enemies! The Bible says, "We love because he first loved us" (1 John 4:19). The power of God is unleashed in human relationships when the message of His unconditional love and acceptance in Jesus Christ is proclaimed.

Ministers Of Reconciliation

What ministry did God give us, according to 2 Corinthians 5:18?

How did Christ reconcile us to Himself (2 Corinthians 5:19)?

What then is the message of reconciliation?

As ministers of reconciliation, what does 2 Corinthians 5:20 say that we are?

Whom does God use to make His appeal to be reconciled?

According to 1 John 4:19, what is the reason that we love, or can become ministers of reconciliation?

What does 2 Corinthians 5:14,15 say controls us?

As a result, for whom do we now live?

How does this change the attitude with which we look at other people (2 Corinthians 5:16)?

How then will we love one another (John 13:34)?

Accept one another (Romans 15:7)?

Forgive one another (Ephesians 4:32)?

The example of David in this chapter testifies today that old resentments are totally gone. The old hatreds have dissipated, and he now feels a genuine compassion for a man whom he once could have willingly killed.

David, as a minister of reconciliation, passed on the forgiveness he received from God. This is a mark of someone who is genuinely growing in grace.

Compassionate Servants

At a seminar, three radiant young women came up and introduced themselves to me. Two of the three ladies were handicapped—one on crutches and the other in a wheelchair. Kathryn said with a laugh, "You could never guess what the three of us have in common. All three of us tried to commit suicide by jumping off the bridge over the river. And now we have formed a ministry together to help other depressed people."

What did the Son of Man come to do, according to Matthew 20:28?

How does Galatians 5:13 say we are to use the freedom that God has called us to?

How does 2 Corinthians 1:3,4 describe God?

What does He do for us in all our troubles?

What then can we do?

Whose comfort do we pass on to others who are in trouble?

What attitude should we have as children of God, according to Philippians 2:3,4?

With the above attitude, how does serving one another in love spell itself out in Romans 14:13?

As servants, are we to please ourselves, according to Romans 15:1,2?

What should our desire be?

Kathryn explained, "Our purpose is to share our life with others who suffer from depression. Though our situations may be different, the problems and pain of depression are the same. Our focus is Jesus Christ, because He is the answer—the only answer."

The picture of these three happy, stable women amazed me. They were peaceful and joyful, and were looking outward to serve the needs of other people. Jesus Christ had not only healed the turmoil of their own souls, but He had also transformed their hearts into tune with His: "The Son of Man did not come to be served, but to serve." This is a mark of someone growing in grace.

Enjoy the Ride

Imagine yourself in a car with two sets of driving controls. You are in one seat, and the Lord is in the other. He says to you,

"Only one of us can drive. The choice is yours. But I love you, and I am committed to your ultimate good. All you have to do is enjoy the ride and let Me drive. I ask you to trust Me, but the choice is yours."

Whose yoke are we to take upon us, according to Matthew 11:28-30?

What will we find for our souls?

How does Matthew describe Jesus' yoke and His burden?

How does this compare to your own burdens?

What does Hebrews 4:1 say we should be careful to not fall short of?

When we enter God's rest, what do we rest from, according to Hebrews 4:9,10?

What did Jesus tell the disciples they were going to do (Mark 4:35)?

How did the disciples react when the storm came up (Mark 4:37-40)?

Who was in the boat with them?

Who had said, "Let's go to the other side"?

Who was responsible for getting them to the other side?

Since Jesus Christ is God, do you think He was able to get the boat to the other side in spite of the storm?

Which was bigger and more powerful, Jesus Christ or the storm?

What does Jesus Christ promise us, according to Philippians 1:6?

Who lives in us in the midst of the storms of life that we face, according to Galatians 2:20?

Who is bigger than the trials and tribulations we face in this world?

How does 1 Corinthians 1:9 describe God, who has called us into fellowship with His Son?

Is He capable of completing the work that He began?

What does 1 John 3:2 say we will be like when we see Jesus?

Are you willing to trust Jesus to complete the work He began in your life?

Growing in Grace, our ongoing experience of *Classic Christianity*, is not "giving it all you've got"; it's allowing Christ to give you all He's got! It is a vital, living relationship with a Person—the Lord Jesus Christ. Let Him drive, and enjoy the ride!

Other Books
by Bob George

Classic Christianity
Classic Christianity Study Guide
Classic Christianity Study Series
   • A Closer Look at the Word of God
   • A Closer Look at Jesus Christ
   • A Closer Look at the Finality of the Cross
   • A Closer Look at the Reality of the Resurrection
   • A Closer Look at Law & Grace
   • A Closer Look at Your Identity in Christ
   • A Closer Look at Faith, Hope & Love
   • A Closer Look at the Truth About Prayer
Classic Christianity Illustrated
Complete in Christ
Living Above Your Circumstances

Additional Materials

Experiencing Victory Over Depression
Video and audiotape series

The spiral into depression begins in our minds—our thoughts. Learn how to avoid the trap of self-pity and despair and experience the reality of Christ as your hope in the midst of *any* hopeless situation.

The New Covenant: Walking in the Fullness of God's Grace
Videotapes

Do you experience fear, guilt, and frustration in life? Certainly, this is *not* what walking in the fullness of God's grace means. In this series, you will learn how to let go of trying to earn God's acceptance and rest in what He has provided you through Jesus Christ.

How to Have a Proper Self-Image
Four audiotapes

If you do not have a proper self-image before the storms of life hit, you can drown in a sea of uncertainty. Discover the difference between a *good* self-image and a *proper* self-image, and understand fully who you are in Christ.

The Battle for Control
Two audiotapes

During the trials of life we are constantly torn between casting our cares on Jesus and trying to control circumstances ourselves. This battle is waged in every believer. In this insightful series, Bob George explain how you can overcome in this battle and live above your circumstances.

For more information, please write to:
Bob George
c/o People to People Ministries
2300 Valley View Lane, Suite 200
Dallas, TX 75234
or call 1-800-727-2828

Other Good
Harvest House Reading

GOODBYE IS NOT FOREVER
by Amy George with Al Janssen

Amy was a baby when the Soviet secret police condemned her father to Siberia. During World War II she witnessed firsthand the horrors of Hitler's Germany, yet also saw evidence that God's grace was at work long before she knew Him.

THE COMMON MADE HOLY
by Neil T. Anderson and Robert Saucy

Neil Anderson, author of the bestselling *Bondage Breaker*, teams up with Robert Saucy, professor of theology at Biola University, to present an extraordinary book on how Christ transforms the life of a believer. At the moment of salvation, all our sins are forgiven—past, present, and future. Christ's righteousness becomes ours. But if this is true, why do we as Christians still sin? More importantly, how can we live righteously? Here, the authors help resolve the confusion about our perfect identity in Christ and our imperfect living in the world.

TOTALLY SUFFICIENT
by Ed Hindson and Howard Eyrich, general editors

Christians and Christian counselors quickly agree that the Bible's message of salvation can lead even the most unlikely people to become children of God. But when it comes to our everyday problems and needs, can we say Scripture is sufficient for *every* counseling situation? More than a dozen professionally trained counselors, medical experts, and pastors who are highly respected in their fields respond to the question that is at the very foundation of the controversy in Christian counseling today. Their answers are enlightening, thought-provoking, and even surprising.